MYSTERIES AND LEGENDS SERIES

MYSTERIES AND LEGENDS

OF NEW ENGLAND

TRUE STORIES
OF THE UNSOLVED AND UNEXPLAINED

DIANA ROSS McCAIN

Guilford, Connecticut

Project editor: Jessica Haberman
Layout: Joanna Beyer
Text design: Lisa Reneson, Two Sisters Design
Map: M.A. Dubé © Morris Book Publishing, LLC

Library of Congress Cataloging-in-Publication Data
McCain, Diana Ross.
 Mysteries and legends of New England : true stories of the unsolved and unexplained / Diana Ross McCain.
    p. cm.
 ISBN 978-0-7627-5059-7
 1. New England—History—Anecdotes. 2. Curiosities and wonders—New England—Anecdotes. 3. Legends—New England. I. Title.
 F4.6.M33 2009
 974—dc22

                                                              2009007033

Printed in the United States of America

10 9 8 7 6 5 4 3 2

To Jack

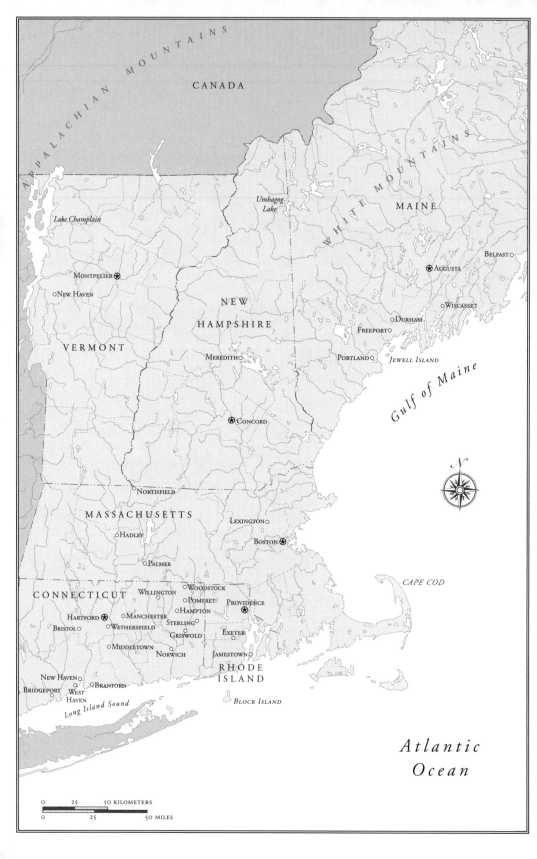

CONTENTS

ACKNOWLEDGMENTS

I am grateful to Globe Pequot editor Erin Turner for offering me the opportunity to write *Mysteries and Legends of New England*. Thanks also to Erin, as well as project editor Jess Haberman, for the steady support and patience they displayed throughout the entire project.

I am indebted as well to the many people who helped me locate and secure illustrations for the book, including Judith Ellen Johnson, Susan Schoelwer, Nancy Finlay, Diane Lee, and Sierra Dixon of the Connecticut Historical Society; Connecticut State Archaeologist Nick Bellantoni; Michael Bell; Nora Monroe; Wes Balla of the New Hampshire Historical Society; Jason Bischoff-Wurstle of the New Haven Museum & Historical Society; Brian Mahoney of the *Lexington Minuteman;* Allene Tartaglia of the Cat Fanciers' Association; and Christine LeFoll of the Godfrey Memorial Library.

INTRODUCTION

MYSTERIES IN HISTORY

When I moved from Ohio to Connecticut in 1977, I had never before set foot in New England. My first job was in the library of the Connecticut Historical Society in Hartford.

One day, not long after I had started working at the Historical Society, a staff member brought up the subject of the Leather Man. As I stood there filing cards in the card catalog—this was, remember, long before the Internet was even a blip on the public's horizon, never mind standard equipment in libraries—I listened with growing skepticism to the story of a strange character who dressed entirely in a crude, homemade suit of leather scraps, who walked the same 365-mile-long circular route again and again for more than twenty years, who never spoke, and whose identity was a mystery that he took to his grave.

This story was so incredibly bizarre that I decided it had to be some kind of prank—perhaps a test of the gullibility of the new hire from the Midwest. But my suspicions were soon dispelled by hard evidence that the Leather Man had been undeniably real. There are photographs of him and dozens of newspaper articles written about him during his lifetime. The Connecticut Historical Society even owns a few small, rare surviving pieces of his leather outfit, including a bag and a glove.

The Leather Man could be considered my introduction to the heretofore-unsuspected weirder side of the region that was my new home. I had always enjoyed reading about ghosts and hauntings—not made-up stories, but accounts of supernatural phenomena that people at least claimed to have experienced—and some of those stories had occurred in New England. But the mystery and legend of the Leather Man, and the many other tales I would encounter over the subsequent decades, were something entirely different.

New Englanders have been depicted classically—or more accurately, stereotypically—as no-nonsense, down-to-earth, reality-based folks who have no time or patience to fritter away on fanciful things. In fact, though, over the past four centuries New Englanders have spawned all manner of odd or bizarre tales that can send shivers down the spine, boggle the mind, and even inspire admiration and awe.

This book includes thirteen of those mysteries and legends. They star vampires and an angel, a ghost rapper and phantom ships, a very cool cat and a giant water monster—and much more. These stories are not works of imagination—at least not entirely. Each tale is rooted in fact (some more deeply than others). For example, for more than a century people have reported seeing *something* they can't identify or explain in the waters of Lake Champlain—exactly what that something is constitutes the mystery.

Sometimes the historical story alone is sufficiently puzzling or creepy or astonishing. Others have been embellished by lively Yankee imaginations, sometimes making it difficult or even impossible to know where fact ends and fantasy begins.

Some of these stories still float on the surface, at least, of the region's identity and cultural consciousness. People's eyes often light up at the mention of the Leather Man. Champ, the monster of Lake Champlain, and New Hampshire's Mystery Stone both enjoy international reputations. Connecticut's revered Charter Oak has been invoked in the names of bridges, roads, businesses, and government programs so broadly and consistently that the phrase at least is familiar to just about anyone in the state—although they likely know only the barest details of the story behind it, if that.

Others of these stories that I encountered over the course of more than thirty years of working in the field of history were once high profile but are no longer, as is the case of one of the first psychics ever to conduct séances. Some, like the legends of vampire activity, didn't circulate very far beyond the communities in which they occurred. And there were fascinating tales, including that of the Angel of Hadley, that I had never heard of until I began my research for this book.

These mysteries and legends are entertaining and some-times amusing. They can also make us think. As you read these chapters, give some thought to what they reveal, both good and bad, about human nature. About how ignorance and fear can make otherwise rational men and women do the unthinkable. About the lengths to which people, individually or as a group, are willing to go to retain a hard-won scrap of independence. About the great significance that connection to a mystery or a legend can bestow upon objects that otherwise have no intrinsic value—a stone, a hunk of wood, a worn-out shoe.

These old stories retain their meaning. But they are pre-sented in this book, first and foremost, to entertain, and some-times to amuse. I hope they will also help restore the brightness of some of the mysteries and legends that add a special color and texture to New England's historical landscape. Whether you are a native, a transplant like me, a visitor, or one who has not yet had the good fortune to personally experience the region's wonders, welcome to the New England of mystery and legend. And enjoy!

CHAPTER 1

THE DARN MAN AND THE LEATHER MAN

Bizarre clothing, obsessive behavior, and impenetrable secrecy characterized two vagabonds who trod the backroads of nineteenth-century Connecticut for decades, on missions whose purpose was known only to them. One was clad in what had begun life as a formal coat but ultimately was mended by him so many times that it became more a tangle of motley filaments than a garment. The other wore an outfit he had fashioned from scavenged scraps of leather crudely sewn together.

More than a century after these two men passed from the scene, questions about who they were, why they dressed in such peculiar and unique fashion, and what motivated each to walk his own set circuit over and over remain among Connecticut's most puzzling mysteries. The tales that sprang up to explain their curious conduct are some of the state's most enduring legends.

The first of these enigmatic strangers took up his self-appointed rounds in eastern Connecticut sometime during the first half of the nineteenth century. By 1860 he had been a regular visitor for some thirty years—always wearing the same coat. When he appeared at a residence along his route, he requested sewing equipment and then set about darning any tears, holes, rips, or rents in the coat. If the woman of the house offered to make the repairs for him, he politely declined. Ultimately, the coat became "simply a mass of twine, yarn and thread," recalled a man who was a boy when he saw the stranger at his family's home in the town of Hampton in 1859. And its wearer had become known simply as the Darn Man, or some variation of that nickname, such as Darn Coat.

The Darn Man appeared in rural northeastern Connecticut every April. He repeatedly walked a rough circuit of at least fifty miles that took him through small towns and hamlets such as Pomfret, Hampton, Sterling, and Woodstock. In January he vanished—where to, no one knew. He returned three months later, like some bizarre migratory bird, to resume his wanderings.

This gentleman—for he displayed the manners of one well bred—typically spent the night at one of the homes along his route. He enjoyed reading the newspapers and magazines to which his hosts subscribed. He knew history and was well informed on recent news.

But to questions about his own identity and origins, the Darn Man gave cryptic, evasive, and sometimes conflicting answers. "If you knew what I know about myself, you would know what I know," he told one inquirer. He once said that his name was George Thompson, originally of Taunton,

Massachusetts. Another time he claimed to be George Johnson, with family in Rhode Island.

However, in conversation the Darn Man did let slip clues about what had launched him on his endless trek clad in the much-mended coat. "Boy, as you grow up, beware of the girls. Don't spend your money on them," the stranger cautioned a youth in the town of Hampton around 1860.

> Don't pay out for a nice wedding suit, especially a coat, for you may be left as I was, to wander about with my wedding coat I avowed to wear until I learned what became of the one whom I had adored, who I am not willing to say went back on me; I am charitable enough to think she was spirited away or lost her mind or perhaps was killed.

Such scarce nuggets of information, combined with observations of the Darn Man's appearance and behavior, formed the nucleus of a romantic legend about who he really was and what had set him on his strange wanderings. While some of the details varied depending on who was doing the telling, the tale was consistent in its fundamentals.

According to the story, the Darn Man was actually Frank Howland, a descendant of *Mayflower* Pilgrims. As a young man living along the eastern Connecticut shoreline, where some versions of the legend say he was employed as a teacher, Howland fell in love with the daughter of a sea captain.

The couple became engaged, so the story goes, and How-land's fiancée sailed to New York to buy her trousseau. But the ship bringing her back to Connecticut and her waiting lover sank, carrying her to a watery grave instead of a wedding ceremony.

Being left standing—perhaps literally—at the altar by such a tragedy reportedly so devastated Howland that he became deranged. He took to wandering the roads of eastern Connecticut, wearing the coat he had donned for the nuptials that now would never happen.

By 1860 the Darn Man's decades of travel had taken a grave toll on the man's body and spirit. He was "tall and gaunt, slightly bent," an observer wrote of him in 1860. "The frosts of sixty winters have changed the once glossy black hair to snowy whiteness," and his face was "pale and emaciated, with lines of sorrow and hardship, with dull meaningless eyes, which always seem fixed on vacancy."

The Darn Man's mysterious, quixotic quest ended three years later. He was discovered, conscious but in critical condition, on Snake Meadow Hill Road in the town of Sterling, just about five hundred feet from the Rhode Island line. Whether he had fallen ill or had been injured in an accident was not reported. By the time he was carried to a nearby home, the Darn Man was dead. Legend says he was buried in Sterling, still clad in the same coat he had worn faithfully for thirty years.

After the Darn Man's death, the legends about him grew to include the circumstances of his passing. On a moonlit June night, according to the tale, the Darn Man was sitting beneath an elm tree in front of one of the houses at which he customarily stopped. When he heard a carriage coming down the road, and the sounds of voices and feminine laughter, he mistook them for the return of the bride he had lost half a lifetime ago. The elderly vagabond raced into the road, calling out, begging his beloved to stop. The horse drawing the carriage, spooked by the man's unexpected appearance, bolted, knocking down the Darn Man and pulling the carriage over him, killing him almost instantly.

Just around the time death ended the Darn Man's decades of wanderings, another mysterious stranger displaying eerily similar behavior appeared on the opposite side of the state. This new character took eccentricity to a whole new level. He wore an entire suit—coat, pants, hat, shoes—made completely of leather. And not the supple leather that one finds in modern garments, but large scraps of leather crudely laced together.

The leather-clad figure walked a 365-mile circuit through western Connecticut and eastern New York State on a strict schedule that took precisely thirty-four days to complete. Unlike the Darn Man, he never took a hiatus from his hike. He tramped his route twelve months of the year, in sizzling heat and bone-chilling cold. By most accounts, he spoke not at all, communicating only in grunts and gestures. Like his predecessor, he came to be known for his odd attire, as the Leather Man.

This stranger who covered an average of ten miles a day on foot, laden with sixty pounds of leather, was not physically imposing: he stood about five feet eight inches tall and weighed approximately 170 pounds. In a small satchel he carried a few meager tools and possessions: an axe, a hatchet, a jackknife, an awl, a frying pan, a handmade tin pipe, some tobacco, and, most intriguingly to those curious about his identity, a French prayer book. He also wore a small crucifix around his neck.

The Leather Man made regular stops at specific homes along his route. He accepted food, drink, and tobacco from the occupants but never slept in any of the houses he visited. His blue eyes regarded everything warily. He preferred to spend the nights in caves or in crude huts or shelters he built out of logs and rocks in the forest.

Residents of the villages and countryside of western Connecticut and eastern New York were likely suspicious of or even frightened by this stranger when he first showed up on their roads. But any such concerns gradually faded with the passage of time.

"Although there is in this State a severe law against tramps, making tramping a State prison offense, no one has ever attempted to put it in force against him," an article in the *New York Times* on August 15, 1884, reported. "The reason is that no one, woman or child, fears him, for all know that he is a harmless creature, and tradition at least has it that he never did and never would harm anybody or anything. He has also an enviable reputation for honesty and sobriety."

The author of an article in the *Penny Press* newspaper of Middletown, Connecticut, concurred. The Leather Man "has been a familiar character or curiosity for some years now, and his stated visits through different towns of the state have made him almost an every day person to a great many people," noted the story, which appeared in the December 3, 1888, issue of the paper. "He is a burden to no one; is inoffensive in his way and prefers the wilds of outdoor life to that of being housed."

By this time, more than two decades into his career, the Leather Man had become the subject of articles in several newspapers, including large urban dailies such as the *Hartford Courant,* the *Danbury News,* and the *New Haven Register,* as well as the aforementioned *New York Times* and *Penny Press.* The most exhaustive published account of the peculiar vagabond's comings and goings was compiled by Chauncey Hotchkiss, a fortysomething clockmaker living in the Forestville section of the Connecticut town of Bristol, one of the stops on the Leather Man's route.

Hotchkiss wrote to people in towns through which the Leather Man passed to compile a detailed list of dozens of communities that were part of his itinerary. Hotchkiss even documented to the hour when the Leather Man passed through Forestville between July 1883 and July 1885. The record showed that the Leather Man arrived in Forestville every thirty-four days, always in the afternoon, always within the same two-hour window of time.

Local newspapers took to reporting the Leather Man's comings and goings like the sightings of a rare bird. The *Penny Press* ran six notices on the Leather Man in 1885, twice that number in 1886, and twenty in 1888.

Like a modern celebrity, the Leather Man became the target of the nineteenth-century version of "paparazzi" who were eager to photograph him, with or without his consent, usually with the intention of selling the images. Photography then being a much more cumbersome process, obtaining a picture without the Leather Man's cooperation was difficult, but not impossible.

In 1885 a teenager in Branford, Connecticut, who had befriended the Leather Man managed to secretly take what one newspaper described as "several good photographs revealing distinctly his [the Leather Man's] features and every wrinkle and stitch in his eccentric costume." It was not long before Leather Man groupie Chauncey Hotchkiss was selling copies for 50 cents each—the equivalent of about $20 today.

Three years later, a Middletown, Connecticut, photographer named Frederick Moore took more than half a dozen images of the Leather Man, apparently without his objection. Moore sold copies at his Middletown studio for 25 cents apiece—about $10 in today's money.

The Leather Man followed his path with relentless fidelity for approximately three decades. The Blizzard of 1888, the worst snowstorm ever to hit the Northeast, put him a few days behind schedule. But the Leather Man refused to allow Mother Nature—or his own failing health, or the actions of well-intentioned strangers—to stop him from pursuing his self-appointed rounds.

In 1888 a growth appeared on the Leather Man's jaw, and it soon became evident to observers that the tumor was an

Copies of photographs of the Leather Man were sold as a kind of postcard souvenir. Middletown, Connecticut, photographer Frederick Moore charged the equivalent of $10 in modern money for a copy of this image he took of the Leather Man a few months before the old wanderer's death in March 1889.

aggressive cancer. By the end of the year, the malignancy had ravaged half of the Leather Man's face as well as part of his neck. He was in such pain that he could eat only bread soaked in coffee, yet he refused any offers of treatment.

Some compassionate individuals decided that the ailing traveler shouldn't be allowed to go untreated, that in fact it was time for him to leave the road and spend whatever small amount of time was left to him in stationary comfort. An article in the *Hartford Courant* on October 11, 1888, advised against such an intervention as "a great mistake."

The *Courant* writer came down on the side of the Leather Man's right to live—and die—on his own terms:

> The man finds his only enjoyment in his absolutely free life. If he were shut up in what people generally would call comfort, there is little doubt that he would fret and pine. . . . [I]f he prefers to trudge on to the last, and then lie down and die by himself as he has lived, who should interfere? It may be that he would pass more easily in that way than surrounded by all appliances of medical treatment and wholly shut off from the way of life he has chosen and which he has followed so many years.

The do-gooders, however, would not be deterred. On December 3, 1888, at one of his regular stops in Middletown, Connecticut, the Leather Man was confronted by two agents of the Connecticut Humane Society, the mandate of which then embraced the welfare of human beings as well as animals. The agents, along with a doctor and the police chief, took the Leather Man into custody, apparently obtaining his reluctant consent with a promise that he would be allowed to resume his travels in the spring. The event made the front page of the next day's *New York Times,* which called the Leather Man "one of the most celebrated characters in Connecticut."

The Leather Man was held temporarily at a local livery stable, where hundreds of people showed up to take a look at the stranger. He and his caretakers then set out by carriage on the twenty-mile trip north from Middletown to Hartford, where arrangements had been made to admit him to a hospital.

However, somewhere along the way to Hartford, the Leather Man apparently had a change of heart about putting himself in the hands of the authorities. He tried to escape— attempting to leap from the carriage in which he was riding, and brandishing a club at his caretakers in an unprecedented act of aggression—but was subdued.

The Leather Man was delivered to Hartford Hospital, where he reportedly told officials that his name was Zack Boveliat, an entirely new piece of information. However, within hours he managed to slip out of the hospital. He headed south, perhaps following the Connecticut River, until he reached Middletown. There he resumed his regular route.

News accounts of the incident caught the attention of the proprietors of Meehan & Wilson's Globe Museum in New York

City. They expressed interest in paying the Leather Man a large salary if he would agree to be displayed in their museum. Their efforts to contact the eccentric vagabond through people who lived along his route were unsuccessful.

As with his earlier counterpart on the other side of the state, the vacuum of information about who the Leather Man was and why he behaved so strangely was filled with a poignant legend of star-crossed love. The Leather Man was, so the legend reported, a native of France named Jules Bourglay. His possession of a French prayer book and reports that he occasionally uttered a few words in French may have been the basis for the legend's identification of that country as his native land.

Young Bourglay, so the tale reported, had acquired a good education despite being the son of a working-class family. He fell in love with a young woman whose father had grown rich in the leather business.

The girl's father opposed the match but offered Jules a chance to prove his worth. The hopeful suitor would work in his prospective father-in-law's leather business for a year. If he proved competent, he would be allowed to pursue his romance.

At first Jules acquitted himself well in the new job. But then he invested a significant amount of his employer's funds in the leather market—and lost it all through bad timing when the market collapsed.

The financial disaster ended Jules Bourglay's hope of marrying his beloved and turned him into a "broken-hearted, shattered-brained creature," in the words of the *New York Times*. Bourglay fled France and somehow ended up in Connecticut, where he commenced trudging his long circuit, possibly as a penance for having failed in business and love. He wore a suit of leather, so the legend says, as a reminder of the source of his sorrow.

The Jules Bourglay legend is first known to have been published in the *Waterbury American* newspaper in 1884. Within a month it was retracted in the same publication, but it proved far too entertaining a yarn to die.

Like the Darn Man, the Leather Man's end came when he was alone. A couple curious to inspect one of the shelters used by the peculiar wanderer found his body in a cave on a farm in Mount Pleasant, New York, near Sing Sing, on March 24, 1889.

Unlike the Darn Man, the Leather Man was not accorded the dignity of being laid to rest in the clothes he had worn obsessively for three decades. He was buried in a shroud in a pauper's grave in Sparta Cemetery in Ossining, New York.

The proprietors of Meehan & Wilson's Globe Museum in New York, who had tried unsuccessfully to lure the living Leather Man into putting himself on display at their establishment, obtained the leather suit from the coroner of Westchester County, in which the renowned vagabond had died. "A life-size figure, an artistic reproduction of every feature of this wonderful old man was made," reported the Globe Museum's promotional pamphlet, "and clothed with the original leather apparel, [they] form for the museum a remarkable, realistic, life-like exhibit of the Old Leather Man."

Eventually, the museum's promotional material continued,

It is the unselfish intention of the proprietors of the Globe Museum, Messrs. Meehan and Wilson, after their patrons have been offered a sufficient opportunity of viewing this interesting counterpart of the Mysterious Leather Man, to present the figure in its entirety to the Connecticut Humane Society, who have always displayed such a praise-worthy interest in the unfortunate Poor Old Leather Man.

Unfortunately, Meehan and Wilson never had the chance to fulfill their purported plan. Most of the Leather Man's suit was destroyed in a fire at the museum. Only a few small articles that once belonged to him—a large leather mitten, a sack, a tobacco pouch, a pipe, his axe—survive in the collections of various historical societies.

A character as mysterious, intriguing, and well known as the Leather Man couldn't die without giving rise to at least one supernatural tale. According to an article in the April 1, 1889, issue of the *New York Daily News,* it was believed that the Leather Man had possessed some amount of money, which he had either hidden in the cave in which he had died or buried in the surrounding woods. No sooner had the old wanderer passed away than hundreds of people flocked to the site of his death, looking for the hidden cash. One of those treasure hunters, a local farmer named Sorrel, conducted his search after dark, using a torch for illumination.

Sorrel returned home after midnight. He hadn't discovered any buried money, but he had experienced a terrifying run-in with what he believed was the Leather Man's spirit! As the *Daily News* article reported, Sorrel's quest had taken him into the Leather Man's cave.

> He said that while he was making his way out of the cave his torch was extinguished. Having no matches, he endeavored to get out without a light.
>
> He was soon confronted by the Leatherman [*sic*], who lit a pile of dry sticks and beckoned to Sorrel to leave at once, which he did with all possible rapidity, running all the way home, a distance of three miles.

Sorrel "is not a drinking man," the *Daily News* assured its readers of the fellow who recounted this "heart-rending story of his narrow escape from the clutches of the Leather Man's ghost." Similar stories were told about some of the Leather Man's other haunts.

For more than 120 years, succeeding generations have kept the mystery and the myth of the Leather Man alive. A Connecticut couple spelunking in one of the caves he used became fascinated with the bizarre character and spent more than forty years collecting all the information they could about him. They went so far as to write to France in search of any confirmation of the Jules Bourglay tale—without any success.

Nothing had been put in place at the time of the Leather Man's burial to indicate the location of his resting place in the Sparta Cemetery. In 1937, thanks to the memory of the daughter of the man on whose farm the Leather Man had died, the site of the grave was pinpointed and at last marked— although by nothing more than a simple iron pipe stuck in the ground.

The iron pipe remained the only indication of the Leather Man's grave until 1953, when a group of people intrigued by his story arranged to have a formal marker placed on the spot. The Jules Bourglay saga had become an inextricable part of the Leather Man's story, and so the inscription composed for the marker read:

Final Resting Place of

JULES BOURGLAY

Of Lyons, France

"THE LEATHER MAN"

Who regularly walked a 365 mile route

Through Westchester and Connecticut

From the Connecticut River to the Hudson

Living in caves in the years

1858–1889

Popular culture has embraced the Leather Man anew. A thirty-minute video about him was produced in 1984. He is the subject of the song "Leatherman," introduced by the American rock band Pearl Jam in 1998. At least two books have been published about the mysterious vagabond who wandered the countryside clad in sixty pounds of leather, the most recent in 2008.

Adding a bit more to the mystery, there is the nursery rhyme that appeared in the first edition of Mother Goose (formally titled *Mother Goose's Melody*) published in the United States in 1785. Although the Leather Man wouldn't make his appearance on Connecticut's rural roads for another seven decades, the poem could have been written about the curious stranger:

One misty moisty morning,
When cloudy was the weather,
I chanced to meet a little old man
Dressed all in leather.

CHAPTER 2

"VAMPIRES" IN THE FAMILY

People long dead and buried sucking the vitality from the still-living sounds like a superstition from medieval Transylvania. But for generations some purportedly no-nonsense New Englanders believed not only that such activity was possible but that it had actually occurred right in their own town. As a result, in at least eighteen documented instances, spread out across all six New England states, frightened men performed variations of the grisly ritual prescribed by folklore to break the supernatural parasite's connection to the living. They exhumed the supposedly life-draining corpse, removed the heart and sometimes other organs, and incinerated them on the spot.

This bizarre scenario inevitably calls to mind the vampires of modern popular culture. But these Yankee "vampires" (contemporary accounts didn't typically use the term until the late 1800s) did not rise from the grave after sunset to walk the earth, nor did they sink their fangs into the necks of their victims to suck their blood. And New England vampires kept it in the family, feeding only on relatives.

The basics of the belief—that the dead could drain the life from living family members and that the only remedy was to disinter, mutilate, and burn the alleged perpetrator's remains—were circulating in New England before the American Revolution. One of the earliest cases to come to light so far occurred in the village of Willington in northeastern Connecticut.

According to a 1784 account by Willington resident (and vampire skeptic) Moses Holmes, the circumstances leading up to this early instance began with "a quack Doctor, a foreigner." This physician claimed "that a certain cure may be had for consumption, where any of the same family had before time died with the same disease."

In the 1700s and 1800s, "consumption" was a catchall term for a variety of lung ailments, most commonly tuberculosis. Tuberculosis was one of the great terrors of the era, killing more people than any other disease. Its victims experienced extreme weight loss, almost as if something were mysteriously consuming their flesh—hence the name "consumption."

Other symptoms included a fever, difficulty breathing, and a wracking cough that often brought up bloody phlegm. The disease could take months or even years to run its course, with the patient growing increasingly thin, pale, weak, and listless, often coming to resemble a living cadaver.

No one knew what caused consumption, and there was no effective treatment. Today we understand that the tuberculosis bacilli are transmitted via coughing, speaking, sneezing, or spitting. A place where people live in close regular physical proximity is an especially hospitable breeding ground for the disease. This was an era when parents with large broods of children typically inhabited houses of a size that made very close contact a fact of life—for example, siblings often slept two or more to a bed—helping to explain why consumption seemed to run in certain families.

The alleged "certain cure" for consumption to which Moses Holmes referred required that the bodies of those relatives who had died from the disease be disinterred. "Out of the breast or vitals might be found a sprout or vine fresh and growing," Holmes continued in his recounting of the "quack" doctor's theory. Any such odd vegetation, "together with the remains of the vitals, being consumed in fire, would be an effectual cure to the same family," Holmes reported.

This macabre ritual was performed in Willington in the spring of 1784 in the hopes of saving a youth from the consumption that had already claimed two of his siblings. Isaac Johnson of Willington had lost his twenty-one-year-old son Amos to consumption in July 1782. His eighteen-year-old daughter Elizabeth had succumbed to the same disease in May 1783. A third child, probably a son named William, was also ill with consumption.

On June 1, 1784, the remains of Amos and Elizabeth Johnson, who had probably been buried in the Old East Cemetery in Willington, were exhumed. Whether Isaac Johnson was present at, approved of, or had even authorized the exhumation of his children was not recorded. Moses Holmes, however, was on the scene to ensure that an honest, objective report was made of what was found in the two opened graves.

Two physicians examined what little was left of the bodies. Moses Holmes reported that "not the least discovery could be made" of any plant growing out of either corpse. He did scrupulously continue to note that "to prevent misrepresentations of the facts, I being an eye witness [*sic*], confess that under the coffin were sundry small sprouts, about an inch in length then fresh, but most likely they were the produce of sorrel seeds which fell under the coffin when put in the earth."

Holmes did not report whether the remains of Amos and Elizabeth Johnson were burned. The grisly ritual apparently failed to have the desired effect. William Johnson died a little more than a year later, in September 1785.

Moses Holmes considered the whole episode to be a cruel display of charlatanism on the part of the foreign doctor. "The public ought to beware of being led away by such an imposter," he warned, so "that the bodies of the dead may rest quiet in their graves without interruption."

Holmes's cautionary account notwithstanding, a dozen attempts to save consumption victims by means similar to those employed in Willington have been documented over the course of the subsequent seventy years. In 1854 one such attempt happened in Griswold, Connecticut, just about twenty-five miles as the crow flies from Willington.

Newspaper accounts from the era provide the basics of the case, which involved the family of Henry B. and Lucy Ray. The couple's twenty-four-year-old son Lemuel had died in 1845 of consumption. The father, Henry, died of the same disease four years later. Another son, Elisha Ray, lost his life to consumption in 1851 at the age of twenty-six.

By 1854 yet a third son, Henry Nelson Ray, thirty-five years old, a factory worker and married father of five, was fighting his own battle with the wasting disease that had taken the lives of his father and two brothers. Some of Ray's acquaintances believed, according to an article in the *Norwich Courier* newspaper, that "*the dead were supposed to feed upon the living,* and that so long as the dead body in the grave remained in a state of decomposition, either wholly or in part, the surviving members of the family must continue to furnish the sustenance on which that dead body fed."

These acquaintances told Henry Ray, according to a report in the *Worcester Aegis* newspaper, "that there was a part of one of those bodies living and preying upon him, and that he would not only fall a victim, but the said body, or the living part, would continue to grow and flourish, until the whole family were swept from the earth." To put an end to this macabre supernatural feeding on Henry, and to protect the rest of the Ray family from it in the future, it was necessary to dig up the three Rays who had died of consumption and to burn "any thing found connected with them not in a state of decomposition."

The editor of the *Norwich Courier* claimed that the proposed ritual was a "strange, and to us hither unheard of, superstition." However, clearly it was essentially the same belief that had led to the exhumation of the Johnson siblings in Willington seven decades earlier.

Henry Nelson Ray's conflicting emotions over the proposed course of action can only be imagined. Guilt and revulsion at disinterring and desecrating his father's and brothers' remains almost certainly struggled with the hope, however slim, that it might bring about a cure. And Henry knew that there was more than his own welfare to consider. The death of their provider would be a calamity for his family, which included a son he had named Lemuel in honor of the dead brother whose corpse would have to be disinterred and violated as part of the contemplated "treatment."

Henry was finally convinced that the procedure should take place. It was performed on May 8, 1854, in the cemetery in the Jewett City section of Griswold. Henry B. Ray and his sons Lemuel and Elisha were disinterred. Henry Ray, dead five years, and one of his sons, probably Lemuel, who had been in the ground for nearly a decade, were discovered to have rotted to an acceptable degree.

But when the heart of the other brother, presumably Elisha, who had been buried the shortest length of time, was cut open, it was purportedly found to contain "fresh blood," according to the *Worcester Aegis.* The men proceeded to build "a large fire in the grave, put the coffin with its mutilated remains into the same, and piled on the fagots until the body that once contained a soul lay in ashes before them."

Most Griswold residents considered the ritual "barbarous," reported the *Worcester Aegis.* It proved as futile for Henry Nelson Ray as it had for William Johnson seven decades earlier. Henry Ray died before the year was out.

The failure rate of this macabre treatment didn't deter other desperate consumption victims from giving it a try. Over the next four decades, there were four more documented instances of attempts to save the living consumption sufferer by digging up and mutilating the remains of relatives who had already succumbed to the disease. The last known case occurred in 1892 in Exeter, Rhode Island, approximately forty miles in a straight line from Jewett City.

Like the Johnsons of Willington and the Rays of Jewett City before them, the family of George and Mary Brown of Exeter was being slowly, inexorably destroyed, one member at a time, by consumption. The first to die was Mary Brown herself, just thirty-six years old, in December 1883. The very next year the disease killed her daughter Mary Olive, twenty.

Around 1890 the couple's son Edwin, a married man in his early twenties, contracted consumption as well. Edwin traveled to Colorado Springs, Colorado, in the hopes that its mineral waters and dry atmosphere would result in some relief, if not an outright cure.

Colorado Springs provided no lasting improvement. By the time Edwin and his wife returned to Exeter, his sister Mercy Lena Brown had also fallen ill with consumption. She died on January 18, 1892, at the age of nineteen, and was laid to rest with her mother and sister in the Chestnut Hill Cemetery in Exeter. Edwin's condition had deteriorated to the point that it seemed he would soon join them in the graveyard.

Once again, frightened people turned to the supernatural for help in fighting a terrifying scourge for which medical science offered no remedy. A letter to the editor in the March 25, 1892, issue of the *Pawtuxet Valley Gleaner* newspaper provided the details of the superstition "regarding the feeding of the dead upon a living relative where consumption was the cause of death." The letter writer reported that "the 'vampire' in question which is said to inhabit the heart of a dead consumptive while any blood remains in that organ must be cremated." The cure had assumed a new, revolting feature: The ashes of the burned heart had to be "carefully preserved and administered in some form to the living victim."

George Brown had lost a wife and two daughters to consumption, and now his son seemed similarly doomed. Nevertheless, he put no stock in the ghoulish superstition that some claimed might save Edwin. At last George was convinced to allow the ritual to proceed, although he was not present when

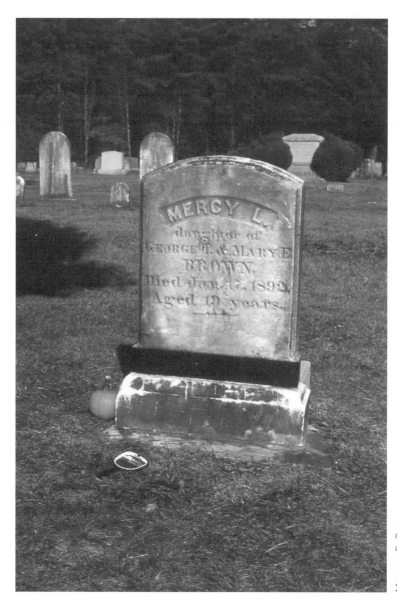

Nothing about Mercy L. Brown's modest, weathered tombstone in the Chestnut Hill Cemetery in Exeter, Rhode Island, hints at the mutilation of her corpse conducted near the site two months after her death in a desperate, superstition-based effort to save her brother's life.

the bodies of his wife and two daughters were exhumed on March 17, 1892.

The remains of the three Brown women were studied by Exeter medical examiner Dr. Harold Metcalf, who acted "under protest, as it were being an unbeliever," according to the letter in the *Pawtuxet Valley Gleaner*. The corpses of Mary Brown and her daughter Mary Olive were, after approximately a decade in the ground, in advanced states of decomposition.

Accounts conflict as to whether Mercy Lena, the most recently deceased, had been buried in the earth or whether her body had been temporarily placed in a crypt to await warmer weather, which would thaw the ground and make digging a grave less difficult. Whichever was the case, Mercy's corpse was examined, and the liver and heart were removed.

Mercy Brown's body "showed some blood in the heart as a matter of course, and as the doctor expected." But Dr. Metcalf's expert opinion that this was not unusual, that Mercy's heart was in a state consistent with the length of time she had been dead, didn't deter the others present from proceeding with their ceremony.

Mercy Brown's heart and liver were burned there in the cemetery. Whether Edwin Brown submitted to the sickening directive that, in order to make the cure certain, "the ashes of the heart and liver should be eaten by the person afflicted" was not recorded.

Yet again, the horrific ritual had been carried out in vain. Edwin Brown lost his battle with consumption six weeks later, on May 2, 1892.

The spate of exhumations, mutilations, and incinerations designed to save the living from the ravages of consumption in New England ended with Mercy Brown. This most likely occurred because medical science had identified the true cause of the disease. The tuberculosis bacillus was discovered in 1882, and the fact that the disease was contagious was established not long afterward. These facts debunked the superstitious belief that the illness resulted from the dead siphoning sustenance from the living.

News of these discoveries may not have filtered out to rural Rhode Island by the time the Brown family started to die off. Even if it had, the claim that consumption was caused by invisible organisms that were passed from one person to another might not have seemed much more plausible than the age-old belief that it resulted from the dead feeding on the living. And it would be decades before a drug that could cure tuberculosis was developed. Faced with such bleak circumstances, some Exeter residents apparently believed there was nothing to lose by trying a folklore remedy, as New Englanders had for more than a century, in the desperate hope of helping a person who otherwise was as good as dead.

CHAPTER 3

THE ANGEL OF HADLEY

The strange figure sported neither halo, nor wings, nor celestial robes. But he is known in New England lore as the "Angel of Hadley" because of the manner in which he mysteriously materialized in that Massachusetts frontier town more than 330 years ago to rally the residents to repel an Indian ambush and save themselves from certain death. Or did he?

First, let's examine the legend, which by the 1870s had "been repeated in one form or another all over the civilized world," according to Connecticut Valley historian George Sheldon. In 1675 southern New England was engulfed by King Philip's War, a gory conflict between English settlers and Native Americans. At that time the Connecticut River Valley was Massachusetts's western frontier. The town of Hadley, which had been settled in 1659 by a group of religious dissenters from Wethersfield, Connecticut, was a vulnerable outpost along the eastern side of that waterway.

On September 1, 1675, so the legend goes, Indians launched a surprise daylight attack on Hadley. The town's residents had come together in their meetinghouse for a special day of fasting and prayer. Although some of the worshippers had brought guns with them to defend against just such a surprise assault, the assembly dissolved into a terrified panic that put them in imminent danger of being overrun and slaughtered.

According to the first published recounting of the story, which appeared in the 1764 *History of Massachusetts, from the First Settlement Thereof in 1628, until the Year 1750,* by Massachusetts lieutenant governor Thomas Hutchinson, suddenly "a grave, elderly person appeared in the midst of them. In his mein and dress, he differed from the rest of the people. He not only encouraged them to defend themselves, but put himself at their head, rallied, instructed, and led them on to encounter the enemy, who by this means were repulsed."

Before the dust had even completely settled, the town's savior simply vanished. "The people were left in consternation, utterly unable to account for this strange phenomenon," Hutchinson reported. The mysterious figure's appearance and disappearance could not be explained by anything other than the sending of some celestial being to deliver the town in its hour of crisis. The remarkable story reportedly spread quickly throughout New England.

The figure who would come to be known in New England lore as the "Angel of Hadley" was, the legend claims, actually William Goffe, a fugitive hiding from the pitiless vengeance of the king of England himself. Goffe had been one of the men, mostly Puritans, who in 1649 signed the death warrant authorizing the beheading of King Charles I of England.

Goffe had successfully commanded troops in battle during the English Civil War, which preceded the king's execution, and during disturbances that occurred in the decade afterward, when England's government was dominated by Puritan leaders, Oliver Cromwell above all. But within months of Cromwell's death in 1658, the beheaded king's son returned from exile. He ascended his father's throne in 1660 as King Charles II and made one of his first and most urgent priorities the hunting down and execution of those men—traitors in his view—who had put their names on his father's death warrant.

William Goffe and fellow regicide (as the signers of King Charles I's death warrant were known) Edward Whalley sought sanctuary among Puritans in New England. In 1664, after three years on the run through Connecticut and Massachusetts, Whalley and Goffe arrived secretly in Hadley. There they spent more than a decade, hiding in the home of Rev. John Russell.

The two regicides' presence in Hadley was a closely held secret, known to only a trusted few. Massachusetts Bay was a Puritan stronghold, but it was also a loyal colony of King Charles II of England. If the fact that regicides were being harbored in Hadley leaked, it would endanger not only Goffe and Whalley but also those who had aided and hidden them. It might even bring the royal wrath down upon the entire colony of Massachusetts Bay.

REPRINTED FROM *OLD HADLEY QUARTER MILLENNIAL CELEBRATION*, 1909. GODFREY MEMORIAL LIBRARY, MIDDLETOWN, CONNECTICUT

A Victorian-era engraving of the Angel of Hadley legend depicts fugitive regicide William Goffe in battlefield commander mode, leading the countercharge against a surprise Indian attack that threatened to destroy the frontier town.

Edward Whalley is believed to have died in the late 1670s and to have been secretly buried in Hadley. At the time of the attack on Hadley in 1675, William Goffe would have been about seventy years old. This would explain what Hutchinson called his "very venerable aspect." Having been in hiding for nearly fifteen years would have accounted for Goffe's strange garments. His experience leading troops in combat back in England would have given him the ability to bring order out of chaos and to inspire the frightened people of Hadley to mount an effective counteroffensive.

Thomas Hutchinson included the story of Hadley's miraculous salvation in a footnote in his *History of Massachusetts* and suggested that the man in question was William Goffe. The source, he said, was "an anecdote handed down" through an old and respected family.

The savior of Hadley formally attained his "angel" status when the story entered the mainstream of New England heritage thirty years later. In his book *A History of Three of the Judges of King Charles I* (1794), Rev. Ezra Stiles of New Haven described the town's mysterious last-minute rescue from annihilation as a "true story" that was "told with some variation in different parts of New England."

Stiles recounted essentially the same story as Hutchinson had. But Stiles claimed that Hadley's "inhabitants could not account for the phenomenon, but by considering that person as an Angel sent of God upon that special occasion for their deliverance; and for some time after said and believed that they had been delivered and saved by an Angel."

Within two decades of the attack on Hadley, the story of "the Angel at Hadley, was . . . universally diffused thro' New England," according to Stiles. "The mystery was unriddled" at last, he wrote, probably in the 1690s. By then both William Goffe and Rev. John Russell, who had sheltered Goffe in his home for so many years, were both dead. England now was ruled by King William and Queen Mary, who had no interest in pursuing their predecessor's old vendetta. It was safe to reveal that a regicide had once been harbored in Hadley.

Ezra Stiles was not only a Congregational minister but also the president of Yale College. One of New England's leading intellectuals, he was a renowned scholar whose academic interests ranged from electricity to Hebrew. For such a distinguished and erudite divine to report the Angel of Hadley tale as fact gave the story great credibility in the public mind and cemented it in New England history.

The story quickly found its way into nineteenth-century popular culture. It was immortalized by artist Frederick Chapman around 1850 in a painting titled *The Angel of Hadley,* which today is on display in the Forbes Library in Northampton, Massachusetts. The tale also was depicted in engravings in nineteenth-century books. Famous and widely read authors, including Nathaniel Hawthorne, James Fenimore Cooper, and Sir Walter Scott, drew on elements of the story in their writing.

In 1874 Connecticut Valley historian George Sheldon set out to debunk the tale of the Angel of Hadley, which by then had been a cherished chapter of New England history for generations. Sheldon laid out his case in an article with the in-your-face title of "The Traditionary Story of the Attack upon Hadley and the Appearance of Gen. Goffe, Sept. 1, 1675: Has It Any Foundation in Fact?" published in the *New England Historical and Genealogical Register.*

Sheldon researched letters and books penned or published shortly after King Philip's War. In none of them did he find any mention of a military confrontation between English settlers and Native Americans at Hadley on September 1, 1675.

The event Sheldon could find that most closely resembled the story of the Hadley attack was an account in Rev. Increase Mather's *A Brief History of the Warr with the Indians in New-England,* published in 1676, the year King Philip's War ended. Mather reported that on September 1, 1675, the people of Hadley had indeed assembled in their meetinghouse. However, they "were driven from the Holy service they were attending by a most sudden and violent alarm, which routed them the whole day after." That was all—no clash of arms, no routing of Indian attackers, no mysterious savior.

Sheldon conceded that "[s]ilence as to this event *might* perhaps have been imposed upon the historians and ministers, who were the chief letter-writers of that period." But he went on to insist that "it is inconceivable that the lips of this great multitude could have been closed, while from the very nature of the case no good reason could be given for silence." He concluded that "the story of General Goffe's appearance either as man or angel, at *any* attack on that town, is a pure romance."

But just as the story told by the historians of one generation—Thomas Hutchinson and Rev. Ezra Stiles—was cast in doubt by the work of a later one, George Sheldon, so Sheldon's effort at debunking the Angel of Hadley legend in turn was challenged more than a century later. In 1987 Douglas C. Wilson wrote in the *New England Quarterly* that he had looked at the same sources Sheldon had examined, but had arrived at different conclusions.

Wilson offered an alternate interpretation that allows for the possibility that William Goffe may well have played a key role in turning back an Indian assault on Hadley. Wilson suggests that the episode was omitted from contemporary writings about King Philip's War by a deliberate conspiracy of silence for the purpose of protecting those who had, and still were, harboring a regicide.

Wilson arrived at his conclusion by pursuing a clue to which Sheldon and previous writers had paid little attention, and by reading between the lines of some of the contemporary accounts. The clue was a letter that Hadley pastor John Russell wrote to Rev. Increase Mather on April 18, 1677, giving his thoughts on Mather's book *A Brief History of the Warr with the Indians in New-England,* which had come off the press the previous year, just weeks after the end of the conflict.

Russell informed Mather that he found "nothing considerable mistaken in your history." But he did express concern over something in Mather's book. Although he alluded to it only vaguely in his letter, he was clearly confident that Mather would know to what he was referring.

"That which I most fear in the matter," Russell wrote, "is lest Mr. B. or some of Connecticut should clash with ours and contradict each other in the story as to matter of fact. Should that appear in print which I have often heard in words, I verily fear the event would be exceeding sad."

Douglas Wilson concluded that what made Russell anxious was Mather's description of an Indian attack on Hadley on June

12, 1676. In his book Mather had given the impression that on that day several hundred soldiers, most from Connecticut, along with a sizable number of Native American allies, had successfully defended Hadley against an assault made on the southern end of town. However, this assault, Mather continued, apparently proved to be only a diversionary tactic designed to draw away the military men so that the Indians could launch a second, "main" attack against the northern end of town, where there were only townspeople to serve as defenders.

Hadley residents somehow managed not only to avoid scattering like sheep in the face of this second assault but also to foil it. According to Increase Mather, after the Indian attackers took up a position in a house, "the inhabitants discharged a great gun upon them" and sent the Indians fleeing for their lives.

How had civilians managed to keep their cool and organize themselves to beat back an Indian ambush? How had they been able to fire a "great gun"—a cannon—with the speed and accuracy to be expected only from someone with combat experience? Could this have been the moment when William Goffe emerged from his hiding place to supply the leadership that saved Hadley from annihilation? And had Rev. Mather, while reporting on the battle in his book, left out any mention of Goffe's participation because he did not want to attract the scrutiny of royal representatives who were looking for the regicides?

Douglas Wilson goes further, citing documents that suggest the Connecticut troops were at Northampton, on the opposite side of the Connecticut River, on June 12, 1676, and thus had no part in defending Hadley against the Indian attack. In his account, did Mather imply that they were in Hadley to provide a plausible alternate explanation for how the Indian assault on the southern end of town had been beaten back?

What did it matter if in his book Mather had indeed fudged and glossed over some facts about what occurred at Hadley in order to protect Goffe and others from royal retribution? What may have had Rev. Russell fretting, Douglas Wilson suggests, was the possibility that some Connecticut official who knew the truth about what had happened that day (possibly including Goffe's emergence and rallying of the townspeople) would publish his version, contradicting Mather's account. This would have the "exceeding sad" results of which Russell wrote—the apprehension and execution of Goffe, and harsh punishment for those who had given him assistance.

Russell's concern might have been sparked by the "Mr. B." he mentioned in his letter. Historians have identified him as Rev. Gershom Bulkeley, who became pastor at Wethersfield after Rev. Russell led his splinter group to a new home in Hadley.

On June 12, 1676, Bulkeley had been with the Connecticut troops in Massachusetts—on whichever side of the Connecticut River they were actually situated. He was in a position to know what really happened that day—and to point out any falsehoods in Mather's published account. Russell's anxiety could have been exacerbated by Bulkeley's reputation for being almost perpetually at odds with just about everyone over any number of issues. Being also a strong supporter of royal authority, Rev. Bulkeley might have been just the kind of man to blow the whole cover story out of spite or royalist principle.

Russell's fears proved unfounded. Perhaps there were enough people in high places in Connecticut and Massachusetts with connections to or sympathy for the regicides to deter Bulkeley from spilling the beans.

Other evidence also points to the possibility that there was some truth to the Angel of Hadley story. After hiding safely in Hadley for more than a decade, William Goffe left the town for good before the end of 1676. If he had indeed played some part in saving Hadley, the report of the mysterious stranger who displayed military expertise to defend the town—a story that had spread by word of mouth throughout New England—might have attracted royal representatives to Hadley, with disastrous results for both Goffe and his abettors should he be discovered there.

Goffe went to Hartford, Connecticut, where he remained in hiding for yet another decade. He died sometime after April 1689 and was buried in secret. According to Rev. Stiles, it was not until after Goffe's death that Hadley residents learned that the wanted regicide had once been hiding in their midst.

Over the course of more than 330 years, the legend of the Angel of Hadley has become even more of a mystery. Was it a real event viewed at the time as a bona fide miracle? Or was it a fantastical tale that falls apart when subjected to skeptical scrutiny? Or was there enough truth to the story that it had to be scrubbed from accounts of King Philip's War to protect Goffe, the people of Hadley, and Massachusetts Bay itself? Those are the questions that have been raised so far—and the future may hold more.

CHAPTER 4

THE MYSTERY STONE

One thing New Englanders have always had more of than anyone could ever want is stones. Whether preparing a field for planting, excavating a cellar, or digging a well, New Englanders even today can count on encountering numerous rocks of various shapes and sizes. Traditionally, these have been used to build the enduring rough walls that have defined property lines and kept livestock penned in for generations.

But a stone that was pulled out of the ground in New Hampshire in 1872 by laborers digging a hole for a fence post was so different that it escaped becoming part of a wall lining a pasture. Instead it became an international curiosity and today is on display as a treasure in the Museum of New Hampshire History.

According to the *History of Merrimack and Belknap Counties, New Hampshire* (1885), the "curious relic" was found about six feet into the earth in a hole being dug near Lake Winnipesaukee, "in the trail of the Indians between Lakes Winnipesaukee and Waukawan." The precise site of the discovery in the town of Meredith has long since been obliterated by construction of a parking lot.

The stone is quartzite, which is not common to New Hampshire. It is approximately the same shape and size as a goose egg. Four inches tall, approximately two and a half inches across, it weighs a little more than a pound. There is a hole bored into each end of the stone.

The stone is dark in color, with a smooth surface into which an assortment of finely detailed symbols or images has been carved. Some of these carvings are literal depictions of unmistakable items: a face, a teepee, an ear of corn. Others are more abstract, their meaning open to interpretation, such as a simple spiral or a crescent moon over two dots and two lines crossed to form an *x*.

When extracted from the earth the stone was so "encrusted" in clay "as to completely conceal all traces of the carving, and only a careful investigator would have discovered its secret," according to the *History of Merrimack and Belknap Counties*. The person who proved perceptive—or simply curious—enough to more closely scrutinize the find was the employer of the laborers who were digging the hole in which the stone was found. He was a local "philosopher and antiquarian" who lived in the town of Meredith, New Hampshire, and went by the appropriately classical name of Seneca Augustus Ladd.

Ladd had grown prosperous through the manufacture of carriages and pianos and later as a banker. He was also a serious

New Hampshire's mystery stone is almost as much of an enigma today as when it was pulled from the ground more than 130 years ago. While modern scientific scrutiny has tentatively dated it to the nineteenth century, the maker and the meaning of the finely carved symbols on the artifact remain unknown.

archaeology buff who had, according to the county history, already amassed "one of the finest private collections of minerals, antiquities, and Indian relics in New Hampshire." The mystery stone—or the "egg," as Ladd dubbed it—immediately became the greatest of his treasures.

A story in the November 1872 issue of *American Naturalist,* the journal of the American Society of Naturalists, recounted the discovery. It reported: "As Mr. Ladd is quite a naturalist, and has already an extensive private collection of relics and specimens, he was delighted with the new discovery, and exhibited and explained the really remarkable relic with an enthusiasm which only the genuine student can feel." The find, according to the *History of Merrimack and Belknap Counties,* "has attracted great attention from the scientific and ethnological world." The Smithsonian Institution reportedly expressed interest in having a cast made of the strange rock.

Seneca Ladd was rumored to have turned down offers to buy the "mystery stone." It was still in his possession when he died in 1892. The stone was passed to one of Ladd's daughters, who in turn held onto it for thirty-five years. At last, in 1927, she gave the strange relic to the New Hampshire Historical Society, which has retained ownership ever since.

Over the years a number of theories have been proffered as to what the mystery stone is and who fashioned it. The 1872 *American Naturalist* article originally conjectured that it was of Native American origin, created for the purpose of commemorating a treaty between two tribes. The *History of Merrimack and Belmont Counties* put forth a different possibility: "It may have been the work of some one living in pre-historic days, as nothing like its fine workmanship has been produced by the Indian tribes of this locality." Other theories have attributed the strange stone to an Inuit craftsman or have deemed it likely of Celtic origin.

Serious doubt was cast on all of these theories when scientific analysis of the mystery stone was conducted in 1994. Results of that study gave reason to believe that the stone had been made by a machine sometime during the 1800s and that the holes in it had been bored by metal tools.

Apart from the information provided by that scientific analysis more than a decade ago, not much more is known about the mystery stone than when it was discovered more than 135 years ago. To this day, no other artifact like it has come to light, nor has anything similar to the carvings on it been found.

So is the mystery stone a work of art? Or is it a pictorial record of some important event? Is it an object intended for use in some kind of ritual? Was it lost or deliberately buried? Or is it nothing more than a carefully crafted fake? That last possibility would seem to deserve at least some consideration, given that the stone was most conveniently "discovered" by a man with a documented passion for acquiring artifacts.

But even if Seneca Ladd did concoct the mystery stone as a hoax, that still leaves a host of unanswered questions. Who actually made the stone, and how, and for what purpose?

Ladd himself never seems to have claimed to know for sure what the stone was, or what process had been employed to create it. And why would he have gone to what must have been a considerable amount of trouble to set up such an elaborate fraud? He did most likely enjoy the limelight that the mystery stone cast on him. But he apparently didn't seek to profit financially from his unique treasure, unlike the hoaxer in the town of Cardiff, New York, who in 1869 secretly arranged to have a ten-foot-tall stone figure of a human being carved. This con artist then buried it and subsequently arranged for it to be "discovered" and exhumed.

The "Cardiff giant" generated a great sensation. Some people believed it to be an ancient statue. Others were convinced that it was literally a petrified giant from biblical times. The maker of the Cardiff giant amassed a considerable fortune, first by charging people a fee to see it and then by selling it for display. Even after the figure was revealed to be a fake, the public happily continued to pay for the privilege of gazing upon it.

Today the New Hampshire mystery stone—whatever it might truly be, however old it is, whoever made it, and for whatever reason—continues to intrigue people around the globe. It is on public view in the Museum of New Hampshire History in Concord, displayed like some precious gem, with mirrors arranged around it so that all facets can be seen.

CHAPTER 5

THE MAINE COON CAT

The Maine coon cat is a living, furry, purring New England mystery. That this popular, unique feline originated in Maine is without question. However, how that came to be has never been answered for certain. Legends allegedly explaining the development of the Maine coon cat have attributed its origins to everything from Viking explorers to a doomed French queen, from a ship captain with the last name of Coon to biologically impossible cross-species breeding.

The Maine coon cat as a distinctive breed is known to have existed at least since the early 1800s. They were originally known just as Maine cats. Sometime around the turn of the twentieth century, "coon" was added to the name for reasons that are not clear.

The Maine coon cat's large, big-boned body is well adapted to the bitter cold, rough terrain, and heavy snow of the land for which it is named. Its long, thick fur serves to keep it warm and to protect it against wind, rain, and snow, as does the long, bushy tail it wraps around its body. Also keeping the cat warm are its ears, which have more fur than do the ears of other breeds. The coon cat's ears are large and have a great range of motion, the better to take in sounds that might alert the cat to prey or danger.

Maine coon cats' paws are large and round, with tufts of fur between the toes—features that facilitate walking on snow. Male Maine coon cats can tip the scales at more than twenty pounds, putting them among the more hefty felines.

The cats that today share living space with millions of Americans are not native to North America. Hence the development of the Maine coon cat must have started *after* the first domesticated cats arrived with the first European humans to visit the continent.

One legend holds that the specific Europeans in question were the Vikings who went ashore at several locations along the North American coast, possibly including Maine, in the early 1000s. The clue to this possibility is the physical resemblance between the Maine coon cat and the Norwegian forest cat. The forest cat is known to have traveled on Viking ships, leading to the theory that a millennium ago some Norwegian forest cats may have slipped ashore and remained behind in the New World. Eventually, they adapted to the specific conditions in Maine and evolved into the Maine coon cat.

Another legend attributes the Maine coon cat's existence to a more recent—and somewhat more far-fetched—historical occurrence. This tale involves a Maine sea captain named Samuel

Clough, who supposedly participated in an attempt to rescue the deposed Queen Marie Antoinette of France sometime after the French Revolution erupted in 1789.

The plan called for sneaking the fugitive queen onto Captain Clough's ship and then sailing to safety in Wiscasset, Maine. In preparation for the voyage, some of the queen's valuable possessions were loaded onto Captain Clough's vessel. These included half a dozen of Marie Antoinette's pet long-haired cats.

However, before the plot could be put into motion, Marie Antoinette was taken into custody by the rebellious French. In 1793 the unfortunate queen would lose her head on the guillotine. As for Captain Clough, he hastily set sail before his part in the scheme was uncovered and before he himself could possibly be arrested.

Captain Clough returned to Maine with his cargo—all the objects that the doomed queen had chosen to take with her into exile, including her cats. The royal long-haired felines supposedly mated with commoner short-haired cats already living in North America. The result, according to lore, was the Maine coon cat. (It is interesting to note, for whatever it might be worth, that in 1790 there was a Samuel Clough living in the town of Durham, Maine, close to Casco Bay.)

If Captain Samuel Clough was not the seafarer responsible for making possible the mix of feline genes that resulted in the Maine coon cat, then perhaps it was Captain Charles Coon. Or cabin boy Tom Coon. Both characters have been put forward as the key players in other tales dealing with the origins of the Maine coon cat.

The legend is essentially the same for both Captain Coon and cabin boy Coon. Each reportedly brought along several long-haired felines on the ships on which they sailed. The cats' task was to catch the rats and mice whose gnawing could inflict major damage to cargo.

When Captain Coon's or cabin boy Coon's ship docked at Maine ports, some of the female cats would go on their own version of "shore leave," during which they would mate with short-haired landlubber felines. Once back at sea, these cats would give birth to litters of kittens that were distinctively different from either parent alone. These were called, of course, "Coon's cats."

Another legend goes beyond the historically improbable to the scientifically incredible conjecture that the mating of felines with wild raccoons resulted in the Maine coon cat. The simple fact that it is biologically impossible for cats and raccoons to cross-breed puts that tale to rest. This myth probably arose because wild raccoons physically resemble the typical Maine coon cat: Both have striped and mottled brown coloring, thick coats, and bushy, ringed tails. (Although brown is the most common coloring, Maine coon cats can also have white, black, orange, blue, or cream fur.) The cats also make distinctive noises that somewhat resemble the chittering of raccoons.

The most logical explanation for the emergence of the Maine coon cat is also, alas, the least entertaining. They are most likely descendants of cats that originally came to Maine with European settlers and that over generations adapted physically to the harsh conditions in their new home.

"For a long time the long-haired cats seemed to be confined mostly to the coast towns and cities of Maine," wrote Maine native Mrs. F. R. Pierce in *The Book of the Cat* (1903). By the end of the nineteenth century, however, they could be found not just throughout Maine but in most states.

"The Maine people having had them so long, it is difficult to arouse any great enthusiasm about them there," Mrs. Pierce continued about the Maine coon cat.

> Not until the craze for long-haired cats struck the West did they think much about selling cats; their very best would be given to their dearest friends. When I think of the number of beauties that I have had given me on my return visits because I would be good to them, it makes me wish for the good old times when the little dears were beyond price in "filthy lucre."

Despite a pedigree shrouded in mystery, and a name that conjures up images of rustic backwoods settlements, the Maine coon cat had become a fashionable pet by the late 1800s. They were competing in formal cat shows in major cities as early as 1878. In 1895 Maine coon cats garnered both curiosity and acclaim at the biggest and most famous cat show held in North America up to that time, at New York City's renowned Madison Square Garden.

"Mrs. Albert Legg's Coonie attracts a great deal of attention, particularly when Mrs. Legg happens to be around to give its history," noted a story about the cat show that appeared in the *New York Times* on May 10, 1895. "Coonie is what is known as a coon cat. He is a large and handsome dark-gray animal, with a fine face, long fur, and bushy tail."

The *Times* article quoted Mrs. Legg as saying that her cat "spends his time hunting when he is at home. . . . He stays hours at a time in the highest tops of the trees. That shows his coon blood." It's not clear from the article whether Mrs. Legg was pulling the reporter's—well, leg—or if she genuinely believed that her cat was part raccoon.

Two hundred cats were entered in that pioneering Madison Square Garden cat show, which, according to the *New York Times* of May 9, 1895, drew "many fashionable people." Selected out of that extensive field of competitors as "Best in Show" was a Maine coon cat.

The champion, a brown tabby named Cosey, was awarded a silver medal and a silver collar. The latter is displayed as a prized artifact at the New Jersey headquarters of the Cat Fanciers' Association, an organization founded in 1906 to document breeds of felines.

The Maine coon cat remained a strong contender for show prizes for another fifteen years. However, in its native Maine, when not being eyed for potential sale, it continued to be appreciated as simply a good pet that needed no fancy awards to validate

This handsome Maine coon cat, named Winter, displays the distinctive thick, luxurious coat; large, furred ears; and big, round paws with tufts of fur between the toes that helped the breed survive in the frigid, rugged, snowy land of its origins.

its value. Mrs. Pierce wrote in 1903 of a handsome Maine coon cat named Tags, owned by a couple in Belfast, Maine, whom she "begged . . . to show him at Boston or New York." The owners steadfastly declined the chance to garner both money and prizes by entering the animal in competitions. The simple reason they gave Mrs. Pierce for their refusal: "Tags wouldn't like it."

But feline aficionados can be as fickle as anyone when it comes to changes in fashion. Maine coon cats gradually lost their preferred status as show competitors to flashier newcomers, including long-haired exotics like Persians. By the 1950s their popularity had plummeted so dramatically that some people claimed—incorrectly—that the Maine coon cat was actually extinct!

Decades of deliberate efforts on the part of Maine coon cat fans brought the breed back from obscurity. The Maine Coon Cat Club was established in 1968, and the Cat Fanciers' Association accepted the breed for championship status in 1976. It has since performed well on the show circuit. By the turn of the twenty-first century, the Maine coon cat was the second most popular breed of cat registered in the United States.

No matter whether its roots extend back to Viking Scandinavia or Revolutionary France, whether it is on a prize-winning roll or relegated to show-circuit has-been, the Maine coon cat is, above all and without question, a true offspring of the Pine Tree State. That status was formalized in 1985, when the Maine coon cat was designated the Official State Cat of Maine.

CHAPTER 6

PREMATURE BURIAL TERROR

Awakening in absolute darkness and total silence to the smell of soil and the sensation of being swathed in a sheet in an enclosed space no bigger than a coffin—because it *is* a coffin—is a gruesome possibility that has haunted humanity for millennia. Americans—New Englanders included—have described their terror of being buried alive through rumors, tales, and legends that circulated by word of mouth and in print. And they have sought measures to ensure that this unthinkable fate would never befall them.

As early as the 1600s, published accounts appeared in Europe of coffins and tombs being opened days or even years after they were closed to reveal a corpse or skeleton in a condition or position suggesting that the person had regained consciousness after interment and had frantically struggled to escape. There were also purported reports of people believed to be dead returning to life in their caskets sometime after they were closed but before they had been placed in the grave or tomb.

By the 1700s such nightmarish tales had increased greatly in number and in the public's awareness. The terror they inspired spawned a movement to alert the public to this alleged threat and to develop ways to cut the number of premature burials as much as possible. The solutions ranged from revised definitions of death to the invention of elaborate alarm systems by which the person interred too soon could signal for help.

At the heart of the fear of being buried alive was the fact that before the latter half of the twentieth century the only sign that a person was unquestionably dead was the onset of decomposition. Few people were willing to subject themselves to the emotional anguish and logistical inconvenience of letting a loved one's corpse lie around the house for several days until it began to decay (for most of this period, there were no funeral homes, so the dead were prepared for burial and laid out at home). As a result, most people were consigned to the earth or, for some of the well-to-do, a tomb, within a day or two after they were adjudged dead.

By the early 1800s, and probably even before, tales of people buried while still alive—or narrowly escaping such a fate—circulated throughout the United States, including New England. The very first issue of the *North American Review* magazine, published in 1815, included this report from Connecticut:

A female supposed dead was nearly buried alive. Animation fortunately returned before the coffin was closed.

Extraordinary Occurrence.

Extrac of a letter from Bavaria.

"We have witnessed here a superb fune rel of the Baron Borost in, a courtier—but the result is what induces me to mention it in my letter. Two days after, the work men entered the mansoleum, when they witnessed an object which petrified them! At the door of the sepulchere lay a body covered with blood—It was the mortal re mains of this favourite of courts and princes. The Baron was buried alive!—On recover ing from his trance, he had forced the lid of the coffin, and endeavoured to escape from a charnal house—it was impossible! and therefore, in a fit of desperation, as it is supposed, he dashed his brains out against the wall. The royal family, and indeed the whole city, are plunged in grief at the horrid catastrophe."

PREMATURE INTERMENT.

We extract the following from the Montreal Sun:

A man of the name of Tessier of the parish of St. Anne, in the district of Three Rivers, supposed to be dead, was carried to Church about twenty four hours after, where his fu neral service was performed. He was then placed in the Charnel House,* which is the ordinary custom in the country during the winter. About 8 days after it became neces sary to open the Charnel House and the cof fin was found open, the feet were out, the hands were torn, the left hand grasped the right shoulder, and the body was turned up on the right side.

* The name of Charnier (Charnel House) is given in this country to a large common grave, where the dead are put during the win ter, so as not to dig a grave for each body.

Columbian.

Cork, July 25. Last wednesday se'nnight a Servant girl, who had been for some days ill of the Small Pox, attended with a fever, to all appearance died, and on Thursday morn ing was interred in a burying ground in this city. Some hours after she was buried, a noise was heard in the grave, which was thereupon immediately dug up, and the body taken out. The girl was alive when the Coffin was open'd, but expired in a few mo ments after: Her body was much bruised and scratched from struggling in the Grave before she was taken up.

THE CONNECTICUT HISTORICAL SOCIETY, HARTFORD, CONNECTICUT

Numerous horrifying reports of people allegedly buried alive and accounts of their frantic and futile attempts to escape were appearing in New England newspapers as early as the mid-1700s. Stories like the ones shown here, from the 1819 Hartford Times *(top left), the 1817* American Mercury *of Hartford (top right), and the 1767* New London Gazette *(bottom), helped keep the fear of premature burial alive generation after generation.*

Such cases seldom happen, but the horrors they excite, leads every one to wish, that such severe regulations for the examination of corpses should be established, that it could never happen.

Not so lucky, according to legend, was one Samuel McDonald, born in Maine in 1771. Sometime after 1815, McDonald left his hometown of Standish in southern Maine to work in the wilderness near Umbagog Lake, which straddles the border of Maine and New Hampshire.

While in that remote area, McDonald reportedly became sick. He lay down in front of a fire, and there he died—or so thought those who discovered him.

When McDonald's sons received the sorrowful news of the tragedy, they covered a hundred miles of rugged terrain in one day to reach the place where their father had died. They buried him temporarily in a box in the forest. The following spring they returned to disinter their father and bring him home for permanent burial.

When the box containing the remains of Samuel McDonald was exhumed from its temporary resting place, the mourners were horrified to discover conditions indicating that he had been buried alive. McDonald "had turned over and during his struggles for liberty he had *gnawed* the boards of his narrow prison-house," wrote G. T. Ridlon in his book *Saco Valley Settlements and Families.*

Fear of premature burial was not confined to the poor or humble or to those who, like Samuel McDonald, died in remote places far from family and friends, all of whom might have real reason to worry that they would be hastily and cheaply interred without a thorough examination to determine that they were truly deceased. No less a luminary than President George Washington, as he lay on his deathbed in 1799, directed that his corpse not be placed in the tomb he had had constructed at Mount Vernon until two days after he had been declared dead—just in case.

The anti-premature-burial activism that had raged in Europe for decades eventually made its way to the United States in the mid-1800s. It was stoked by popular fiction such as Edgar Allan Poe's 1844 short story "The Premature Burial."

"To be buried while alive is, beyond question, the most terrific of these extremes which has ever fallen to the lot of mere mortality," Poe wrote. In nightmare-inducing detail, the master of horror described what such a fate would feel like:

No event is so terribly well adapted to inspire the supremeness of bodily and of mental distress, as is burial before death. The unendurable oppression of the lungs—the stifling fumes from the damp earth—the clinging to the death garments—the rigid embrace of the narrow house—the blackness of the absolute Night—the silence like a sea that overwhelms—the unseen but palpable presence of the Conqueror Worm—these things, with the thoughts of the air and grass above, with memory of dear friends who would fly to save us if but informed of our fate, and with consciousness that of this fate they can never be informed.

The fear reached fever pitch in the United States in the late 1800s. Magazines and books, some of the most influential of which had connections to Boston, filled with gruesome accounts of premature burial found an eager audience.

In 1883 Dr. Moore Russell Fletcher, a Boston physician, published the alarmingly titled *One Thousand People Buried Alive by Their Best Friends.* In 1895 the Occult Publishing Company of Boston brought out Dr. Franz Hartmann's *Buried Alive,* which present-day author Jan Bondeson has derided as a "deplorable volume" that "contained a greater proportion of horrid stories than any previous work in the English language."

The 350-page-plus book *Premature Burial and How It May Be Prevented,* by William Tebb and Dr. Edward Perry Vollum, was published in 1896, and a second edition came out in 1905. Dr. Vollum had a bit of firsthand experience with the phenomenon that was the subject of their book. As a boy he had been presumed dead after a drowning accident, and his body was placed in a morgue. When he regained his senses, he found himself in a room full of cadavers awaiting burial—an undoubtedly and understandably traumatic experience, especially for a child.

Certainly not all New Englanders read Edgar Allan Poe or any of the lengthy, supposedly nonfiction treatises written by physicians on the subject of being interred alive. But they could still be exposed to unnerving reports of premature burial simply by skimming the daily newspapers.

The April 2, 1858, issue of the *Berkshire County Eagle,* published in Pittsfield, Massachusetts, contained an item titled, with impressive understatement, "Buried Alive—A Distressing Case." It described an incident that took place in the town of Holland in western New York State in which a minister traveling to a meeting spent the night in the house of a fellow clergyman who was going to the same meeting.

The visiting man of the cloth had a fit during the night, and according to the newspaper report, "it was supposed he had died." The still-living minister, "being in a hurry to get to the meeting," had his presumably deceased colleague buried the following day. When he got back from his conference, he communicated to the dead minister's friends the sorrowful news of his death, as well as the details of his interment.

The deceased minister's friends soon came to take his remains back home for burial only to discover, when the body was exhumed, shocking evidence that he had been buried alive. "The cover of the coffin was split, and his shroud was completely torn off and turned nearly on his face," the account in the *Berkshire County Eagle* reported grimly.

Another example of journalism's contribution to the fear of premature burial was an article that appeared in the Fitchburg, Massachusetts, *Daily Sentinel* on October 30, 1890. It reported that in New Philadelphia, Ohio, a man was pronounced dead of an overdose of morphine. He was buried two days later. The man's brother arrived in New Philadelphia three days after that and asked that he be allowed to look one last time upon his late sibling.

"When the coffin was opened," the *Daily Sentinel* item reported, "it was found that the supposed dead man had been in a stupor and had come to life in the casket. His face was scratched and the glass in the coffin was broken."

One of the responses to the public's dread of this horrific possibility was the development of caskets equipped with special features that would alert people aboveground if a person had been accidentally buried alive. These distress signals would lead, it was hoped, to a timely exhumation, so that premature burial did not become premature death.

More than a score of U.S. patents were taken out for these so-called security coffins. They offered a variety of options. Most, however, were designed to be activated by motion—a twitch, a jerk—that a prematurely buried person might make even if unconscious. This usually involved attaching strings to the interred person's fingers or toes, so that any movement, voluntary or involuntary, would trigger the mechanism.

Some security coffins were equipped with tubes that connected the interior of the buried casket to the surface. These would purportedly allow the prematurely interred person to breathe until rescued. Others featured not only bells but also other alarms, such as flags, which the coffin's still-vital occupant could use to signal to those aboveground.

As technology advanced, newer and literally flashier warning devices, including lights and a telephone, came on the market. One security coffin model featured not only a bell alarm but also a supply of food and wine to sustain the prematurely buried person should assistance be slow in arriving. It was also equipped with a ladder so that the person, if strong enough, could climb out of the grave. Other security coffins were also designed to allow the not-really-dead to effect their own escape rather than waiting for help to arrive. One was fitted with springs that would cause the coffin lid to snap open at the touch of a living occupant.

Evidence of one New Englander's absolute determination not to experience the terror of being buried alive can still be seen today. The location is Evergreen Cemetery in New Haven, Vermont.

Dr. Timothy Clark Smith was not a credulous bumpkin but a well-educated, well-traveled physician, merchant, and former diplomat. Born in Monkton, Vermont, in 1821, he was a member of the class of 1842 at Middlebury College. Records do not indicate whether he graduated. He received his degree in medicine from the University of New York in 1855.

Dr. Smith spent more than a decade serving as U.S. consul in Odessa, Russia, and another five years of government service in Romania. Eventually he retired to his native Vermont.

Dr. Smith died suddenly and unexpectedly on February 25, 1893, in Middlebury. After eating breakfast at the hotel where he lodged, he strolled over to the stove in the establishment's office—and abruptly dropped dead at the age of seventy-one.

Dr. Smith apparently harbored a fear of being interred alive. One story claimed that during his international travels the physician had learned about the disease known as sleeping sickness. This knowledge led him to fear that, however unlikely, he might fall ill with it and be incorrectly pronounced dead.

Like George Washington, Dr. Smith dealt with the possibility of being buried alive by directing that a certain period of time be allowed to pass before he was consigned to the grave—or, as it happened in his case, the tomb. But that was just the first step in Dr. Smith's plan to avoid the horrors of premature entombment.

One of Dr. Smith's sons reportedly traveled back to Vermont from Iowa to oversee construction of a crypt designed by his father. The subterranean tomb consisted of two chambers—one for Dr. Smith, the other for his wife—and stairs leading out of it and up to the surface. But most curious, and apparently most important for the physician's plan to ensure that he was not interred prematurely, was the long shaft in the earth that extended from the interior of the casket to what appears to be a square glass "viewing" window on the surface.

Exactly what purpose Dr. Smith intended this feature of his tomb to serve is not clear. Did he expect that visitors might peer down into the shaft and, if he had indeed been buried prematurely, perceive his situation and arrange for him to be rescued? Or did he have it installed so that, should he awaken six feet under, he would be able to see to the surface and perhaps catch the eye of some passerby who would summon help?

Rumors also circulated that Dr. Smith had been buried with a hammer and chisel that he could use to chip his way out of his tomb if he revived, or with a bell that he could ring to summon help.

There is no evidence that Dr. Smith had occasion to use the special features of his custom-made tomb, or that he was anything but stone-cold dead when he was placed in it. The window atop the shaft is still there. Although more than a century of condensation and vegetation growth has made it impossible to see to the bottom of the shaft, legend says that it was once possible to view Dr. Smith's skeleton with his unneeded tools of escape.

In the century or more since Dr. Smith's death, science and historical research have largely explained the premature burial tales that haunted so many people. Many of the stories were rumors or outright fabrications that were recycled by writer after writer, often put in a new setting or with different details. Some of the signs that were once considered evidence that a person had been buried alive are now understood to be the result of the natural process of decomposition. Contorted facial features and limbs, or even sounds heard emanating from inside a closed coffin, can be attributed to the biological processes that a body naturally undergoes after death. These include a period when a corpse becomes temporarily rigid, the contraction of skin, and the production of gases that often build up inside the body during decomposition, causing it to shift or make sounds. Horrifying cases like that of Samuel McDonald may be explained by the shifting of the body when the coffin is placed in the grave or by rodents' gnawing on the coffin and on the corpse itself.

That is not to say that premature burials have never happened. More than a few reports have been supported by solid eyewitness testimony—and sometimes even the statements of those who had been buried alive. However, the increasing prevalence, at least in the United States, of autopsies, embalming, and cremation have greatly reduced the chances of someone's being buried alive—and have eliminated whatever minimal reason there might have been for an elaborate fail-safe setup like Dr. Smith's.

A gruesome aside: For decades during the nineteenth century, enormous special buildings were constructed in Germany for the specific purpose of housing corpses until decomposition set in, at which point death could be deemed a certainty. The presumably dead people usually had strings attached to their fingers that would ring a bell if the supposed corpse moved. The ringing would alert the attendants to check whether the person had indeed been incorrectly declared dead. No instance in which this precaution saved a person's life has been found.

CHAPTER 7

PHANTOM SHIPS

In the nearly four centuries since Europeans first settled New England, countless sailing ships have set out from the region's ports, slipped over the watery horizon—and vanished. Most were never seen or heard of again, their fates forever unknown. But legend tells of more than a few such lost vessels that returned in spectral form—sometimes more than once.

One of the very earliest of these mysterious ships sailed from New Haven, Connecticut, in 1646. New Haven had been founded just eight years earlier by English immigrants with backgrounds in trade, which they had planned to continue pursuing in their new frontier home. But the commerce they conducted, primarily with other New World colonies, didn't turn out to be as profitable as they had hoped.

Finally, New Haven leaders decided to bet everything on one last throw of the metaphorical dice. They would dispatch directly to England a "Great Shippe" laden with an extraordinarily valuable cargo to trade. That they determined to do so despite powerful evidence that the odds were against them was a measure of the depth of their desperation.

The vessel that would carry the hopes of an entire fledgling colony was brand-new, built in neighboring Rhode Island. These facts were not necessarily favorable to the enterprise's chances of success. The seaworthiness of the Great Shippe—not its name, but the term by which it was referred to in the records—had yet to be tested. This wintertime transatlantic trip would be her maiden voyage.

Even worse, the Great Shippe apparently was not particularly well constructed. Her own captain considered the vessel "so waity" that he gloomily predicted "she would prove their grave."

The Great Shippe set sail on this critical mission in January 1646. It carried a valuable cargo that included wheat, hides, and beaver pelts, along with approximately seventy passengers and crew.

In pronouncing a benediction upon the departing vessel, New Haven founding father Rev. John Davenport prayed, "Lord, if it be thy pleasure to bury these our friends in the bottom of the sea, they are thine; save them!" Following that less-than-optimistic send-off, the Great Shippe wound its way through a three-mile-long channel that had been chopped out of the ice covering New Haven Harbor before it could at last reach open water.

The time it took for a sailing ship to cross the Atlantic in the 1600s could vary greatly. The voyage could take anywhere from a few weeks to a few months, depending on a host of uncontrollable and unpredictable factors, including the winds, the weather, the skill and experience of the crew, and the soundness of the ship. But when an entire year passed with no word from or about the Great Shippe, the only rational conclusion was that the forebodings of the shipmaster and the pastor had been realized. The vessel, its valuable cargo, and all the souls on board had been lost at sea.

New Haven residents turned from praying for the Great Shippe's safe return to beseeching God to "let them hear what he had done with their dear friends, and prepare them with a suitable submission to his Holy Will," according to Rev. James Pierpont, who became pastor of the New Haven Congregational Church in 1685. Their prayers reportedly were answered in the summer of 1648 in a most phenomenal manner. The extraordinary event was documented for posterity by Rev. Cotton Mather of Boston in his 1702 book *Magnalia Christi Americana* (*The Ecclesiastical History of New England*).

Rev. Mather, who was one of colonial New England's leading scholars, had asked Rev. Pierpont to gather information about the saga of the Great Shippe for inclusion in *Magnalia Christi Americana*. Pierpont's response, as published in Mather's book, included his "relation . . . which I have received from the most credible, judicious and curious surviving observers" of an "apparition of a ship in the air" in 1648 in New Haven Harbor.

In other words, Rev. Pierpont interviewed eyewitnesses to the appearance of a phantom vessel that they believed to be the Great Shippe. Although the event had occurred nearly half a century before the late 1600s, when he began soliciting accounts, at least some of the witnesses with whom he spoke would have been only in their fifties or sixties, and their memories of that remarkable event remained sharp and clear.

On a June day in 1648, as Rev. Pierpont recounted in the pages of *Magnalia Christi Americana,* a powerful thunderstorm pounded New Haven. The weather cleared, and then, about an hour before sunset, a vessel of the same size and configuration as the long-lost Great Shippe "appeared in the air coming up from our harbour's mouth, . . . seemingly with her sails filled under a fresh gale, holding her course north, and continuing under observation, sailing against the wind for the space of half an hour."

Pierpont continued his account of what he had been told about that unforgettable afternoon:

> Many were drawn to behold this great work of God; yea, the very children cryed [*sic*] out, *There's a brave ship!* At length crowding up as far as there is usually water sufficient for such a vessel, and so near some of the spectators, as that they imagined a man might hurl a stone on board her, her main top seemed to be blown off, but left hanging in the shrouds; then her mizen top; then all her masting seemed blown away by the board: quickly

after the hulk brought unto a careen, she overset, and so vanished into a smoaky [*sic*] cloud, which in some time dissipated, leaving, as everywhere else, a clear air.

The admiring spectators could distinguish the several colours of each part, the principal rigging, and such proportions as caused not only the generality of persons to say, *This was the mould of their ship, and this was her tragick* [sic] *end.*

Rev. John Davenport, who more than two years earlier had given the Great Shippe such a pessimistic send-off, considered the apparition a message from heaven intended to give the people of New Haven closure. According to Pierpont's account in the *Magnalia Christi Americana,* Davenport declared that "God had condescended for the quieting of their afflicted spirits, this extraordinary account of his sovereign disposal of those for whom so many fervent prayers were made continually."

Cotton Mather put his personal endorsement on Davenport's account, writing in *Magnalia Christi Americana:* "Reader, there being yet living so many credible gentlemen, that were eye-witnesses of this wonderful thing, I venture to publish it for a thing as undoubted, as 'tis wonderful."

Vouched for by eyewitness reports that were published in a pioneering book by one of colonial New England's leading clergymen, the "Phantom Ship" (as the specter vessel came to be called) was assured a secure spot in the region's lore. It has inspired creative figures over the intervening centuries. Henry

Wadsworth Longfellow memorialized it in verse. The nineteenth-century landscape artist Jesse Talbot depicted it in paintings, and more recently it was represented by a metal sculpture erected in the 1980s in New Haven.

After that one spectacular sighting, New Haven's Great Shippe was never spotted again. But some New England phantom vessels have been reported to make encore appearances that have occurred over the span of a century or more. One of these repeat performers is the *Dash,* a Maine ship that lore claims was sighted during World War II, more than 125 years after it vanished.

Built in Freeport, Maine, and launched in 1813, the *Dash* was dramatically different from the New Haven Great Shippe in critical ways. Not a clumsy tub, the *Dash* had been carefully crafted for speed and maneuverability, for she was destined to serve as a tool of war.

The *Dash* came off the ways at Freeport during the War of 1812, which pitted the United States' small naval force against that of Great Britain, the world's greatest maritime power. In an attempt to even the odds, the United States turned, as it had during the American Revolution, to privateering. In this practice, the government licensed privately owned and operated ships to hunt down and capture enemy vessels, both military and civilian.

Privateering—considered "legalized piracy" by some—was an extremely dangerous business. But it also offered the potential

*New Haven residents marvel at the specter of the Great Shippe,
of which no news had been heard since it set sail in January 1646,
in* Vision of the Phantom Ship, *painted by Jesse Talbot
sometime between 1850 and 1875. Rev. Cotton Mather of Boston
claimed that "so many credible gentlemen" had been "eye-witnesses
of this wonderful thing," that he considered it "undoubted"—
that is, he believed it to be fact.*

for huge, fast jackpots. Any ship seized by a privateer would
be sold along with its cargo. The privateer's crew, owners, and
investors would share in the proceeds.

While privateers were pursuing profit, they were also
serving the American war effort. By seizing enemy ships, they
disrupted trade and supply lines. They frequently brought back
goods desperately needed by the United States' own armed
forces. Because British warships had to chase privateers, they

were often diverted from the business of engaging the enemy in combat or were tied up escorting private British merchant and passenger vessels safely to their destinations.

The *Dash* made several voyages, slipping through Great Britain's blockade of the New England coast on trading missions to the West Indies, before it was commissioned as a privateer on September 13, 1814. Notices in Massachusetts and Maine newspapers chronicled her subsequent daring and often profitable exploits.

In October 1814 the *Dash* brought a British privateer into Portland. Just a month later the *Dash* brought a schooner with a cargo of fish into New Bedford, Massachusetts. During the latter voyage, the *Dash* had spent two days evading pursuing British frigates.

The *Dash* quickly returned to the hunt. The ship went back to Portland in early January 1815, having captured no fewer than five enemy vessels. Their combined cargoes of fish, sugar, rum, cotton, rice, wine, copper sheeting, and other goods had a total estimated value of $120,000—worth well over $1.5 million in today's money. In just four months the *Dash* had compiled a phenomenal record of success as a privateer, capturing fifteen prizes without ever losing a man.

The *Dash* set sail once more on January 21, 1815, in the company of another privateer, the *Champlain*. Commanding the *Dash* on this voyage was Captain John Porter, whose family owned the Freeport shipyard in which the *Dash* had been built.

Captain Porter, just twenty-two years old, left behind a wife pregnant with the couple's first child.

Reports on the size of the *Dash*'s crew on this voyage vary widely, ranging from thirty-seven to sixty men. Included among that number were two of Captain John Porter's brothers, Ebenezer Porter, twenty-four, and Jeremiah Porter, eighteen. Thirteen other Freeport men were also on board.

When the *Champlain* returned to port—without the *Dash*—it was to tell a story that gave every reason to believe the *Dash* would never be seen again. The two ships had been more than a day out from Portland when a powerful gale developed. The *Champlain* reversed course to avoid the storm, but the *Dash* continued on. It was assumed that Captain Porter had made a serious mistake in judgment that resulted in the ship's foundering on the shoals of the Georges Bank and sinking to the bottom of the Atlantic.

In a bit of tragic irony, it turned out that the war in which the *Dash* served as an American weapon was already over. The conflict had ended when representatives of the United States and Great Britain had signed the Treaty of Ghent on December 24, 1814, in Europe. In an era before even telegraph communication existed, news, no matter how momentous, could travel no faster than the ship carrying it. Thus word of the war's end didn't reach Maine until after the *Dash* had set sail on her last voyage.

That so splendid a ship with a perfect track record of success in such a risky line of work, carrying more than a dozen local young men, should vanish was a particularly grievous blow. And those factors gave the *Dash* all the makings of a great ghost ship.

Local fishermen began to report sighting the *Dash* at various spots in Casco Bay. The vessel always appeared suddenly, without warning, in a dense fog. With its sails unaccountably billowing, the ship, its name clearly readable, would be making good speed. Sometimes crewmen were visible.

A legend sprang up to explain the *Dash*'s repeated materializations. When a relative of a *Dash* crewman died, so the story went, the vessel would reappear to transport the newly departed person to eternity. But such a mission would not explain all of the spectral *Dash*'s returns, such as when the ghost ship allegedly reappeared in Casco Bay 127 years after it originally vanished.

Casco Bay in August 1942 was buzzing with all manner of vessels of the U.S. and British navies, united to defend the coast against their common enemy, the Axis powers, with which the United States had been at war for eight months. Casco Bay was being protected by the new electronic detection system called "radar."

One foggy August afternoon, alarms suddenly went off, alerting Casco Bay's defenders to the presence of an unidentified and unauthorized intruder. Legend reports that a couple who had rowed to a small, secluded island for an illicit rendezvous unexpectedly found themselves with front-row seats for what then allegedly transpired.

The lovers reportedly observed an early-nineteenth-century sailing ship, displaying the name *Dash,* as well as its crew, sail past, chased by American and British vessels. Before its pursuers could overtake it, the *Dash* stopped and simply floated away into the mist. That World War II appearance was the last reported sighting of the *Dash*—to date.

A vessel doesn't have to vanish to become a regular specter off the New England coast. The ship *Princess Augusta* reportedly came to a tragic end, smashed to splinters on the rocky shore of Block Island in 1738. However, the murky circumstances leading up to and surrounding that event have resulted, according to legend, in repeated reappearances of the lost vessel, engulfed in flames.

The *Princess Augusta* reportedly set sail sometime in 1738 from the port of Rotterdam in the Netherlands. It was carrying 350 German passengers bound for Philadelphia. At some point in the telling and retelling of the tale, the *Princess Augusta* came to be more popularly known as the *Palatine,* possibly because its passengers were from the Palatinate area of Germany. Whatever the explanation, *Palatine* is the name that has been attached to the ship in popular lore for at least the past 150 years.

Sometime before the *Princess Augusta* arrived within sight of the North American coast, death and devastation swept through the ship. There were conflicting reports about what exactly had transpired during the voyage.

Disease unquestionably killed many of the passengers and crew, including the captain. But there were also stories that the crew had abused, starved, and mistreated the passengers, extorting all manner of valuable possessions from them in return for food. By the time the *Princess Augusta* had crossed the Atlantic, only an estimated 150 of the 350 people who had started the voyage were still alive.

By the night of December 26, 1738, the *Princess Augusta* had veered drastically off its intended course for Philadelphia. The vessel was anchored about a dozen miles off the Rhode Island coast, when a howling snowstorm with gale-force winds blew in. The crew tried to navigate the ship between Long Island and Block Island, but the *Princess Augusta* ended up running aground on Sandy Point at the northern tip of Block Island.

Alternate versions of what happened that stormy December night claim that the *Princess Augusta*'s grounding on the shore of Block Island was no accident. One bit of lore blames a group of heartlessly avaricious residents of Block Island. These greedy opportunists set fires that they hoped the crew of the *Princess Augusta,* navigating in darkness and foul weather, would mistake for beacon lights that they could use to guide them to safe harbor. The deception worked, and the unwitting crew steered the crippled ship right onto Sandy Point.

Others contend that it was the crew of the *Princess Augusta* who deliberately wrecked the ship. They did so to hide any physical evidence of their abuse and extortion of the passengers during the voyage. By some accounts, they torched the ship to conceal their crime.

There are multiple contradictory accounts of what happened to the *Princess Augusta* after it came to rest on Block Island. Testimony taken from some of the crew members contended that after the ship struck the shore, the captain urged the passengers and crew to salvage whatever they could of the vessel itself and its cargo "both before and after She broke to Pieces."

According to another story, when dawn brought enough light, some Block Islanders swarmed over the beached wreck, eager to "help" the suffering passengers evacuate the ship quickly—so quickly that they had no time to gather up any of the belongings left to them after the crew's plundering. Once the ship was evacuated, the "rescuers" returned to the *Princess Augusta,* pillaged it of every object of value they could find, and then set the wreck on fire to hide their larceny.

What was the fate of the *Princess Augusta*'s passengers and crew? According to one account, they were rescued by compassionate residents of Block Island. These local folk took the wretched survivors into their homes, fed them, and provided them with medical care.

Unfortunately, most of those who managed to come ashore on Block Island were too weakened with disease and deprivation to survive long. Almost all of them died as a result. Another variation on the story claims that the Block Island "wreckers" killed the survivors to ensure that there would be no witnesses to their plunder of the wreck. However these doomed immigrants met their deaths, they were interred at a spot identified today by a marker that says simply PALATINE GRAVES.

Not surprisingly, Block Island residents contended that the account of their compassionate care of shipwrecked strangers told the true story. Off the island, the more colorful tale of deceit, theft, flames, and death—accidental or homicidal—gained popularity.

Some decades after the loss of the *Princess Augusta,* "a strange, unearthly phantom light appeared around the north end of the island near the spot where the *Palatine* was destroyed," reported an article in the August 15, 1885, issue of the *New York Times.* "It was always seen at night and before a dark, easterly storm. That light has been seen with greater or less frequency ever since. It is the ghost of the *Palatine,*" supposedly appearing in the flames that had consumed it.

In an article in the March 23, 1878, issue of the *Newport Mercury,* ninety-year-old Benjamin Congdon, who had spent his boyhood close to Block Island, claimed that he had witnessed the specter of the blazing *Palatine* at least eight times over the course of his life. "In those days nobody doubted her being sent by an Almighty power to punish those wicked men who murdered her passengers and crew," Congdon claimed.

Block Islanders didn't deny the phenomenon of the phantom light. But they insisted that it was nothing more than a harbinger of bad weather and had nothing to do with whatever sad fate had befallen the *Palatine.*

In 1867 the poem "The Palatine," by renowned poet John Greenleaf Whittier, was published in *Atlantic Monthly* magazine. Whittier lived all his life in Massachusetts and New Hampshire, many miles from Block Island. His recounting of the legend included the deception, crime, and cruelty that supposedly lay behind the reappearance of the ship's specter.

Block Islanders were not happy about their ancestors' being portrayed in a national publication as vicious wreckers, plunderers, and murderers. When their discontent was brought to Whittier's attention, the poet explained that he had based his work on the "current tradition on the mainland" as it had been told to him by a Rhode Islander.

The *Princess Augusta's*—or *Palatine's*—spectral appearances have followed no apparent predictable schedule, nor have they been triggered by any known events. The phantom ship was spotted, for example, during the winter of 1873–74, after which more than a decade passed before another sighting was reported—this one during the summer.

Block Island residents are not the only ones who have reported seeing the specter of the *Palatine.* In 1885 a Philadelphia man by the name of Montgomery, who had come to Block Island on a fishing vacation, was standing on the porch of his lodging at Clay Head around 11:00 p.m. He was "admiring the ominous majesty" of a storm when suddenly he spotted an "eerie blaze," according to the August 15, 1885, *New York Times* article.

The vision "lasted about 15 minutes, and the gentleman was converted from a skeptic to the truth of the phantom shimmer into a profound believer in the yarn," reported the *Times*. "Fully 10 people besides Mr. Montgomery saw the phantom, and their descriptions are very vivid."

Those descriptions were of a "whitish flame, pyramidal in shape, and very much the size and form of a large ship under full sail," reported the *Times*.

> The flame seemed to shoot out of the water off Southeast Point, and impelled doubtless by the easterly wind, moved steadily and rapidly across the harbor toward Sandy Point, and there sank or faded out of sight. During at least five minutes of the time the silent flame towered aloft with sufficient vigor to lighten up the land. . . . At this point it was a very beautiful light.

Apart from whatever strange things were happening out on the water, some Block Island residents believed that the houses to which the *Palatine*'s survivors were taken were haunted. In a legend that spun off from the original tale, even an inanimate piece of the ship was considered to be possessed.

According to this story, Block Islanders scavenged from the ship a piece of lignum vitae wood, prized for its hardness and durability. Out of this they fashioned a mortar—a bowl about fourteen inches high and ten inches across—in which corn was ground into meal by use of a pestle.

However, local lore claims that the mortar demonstrated a mind of its own—as well as the power to move. Sitting before the hearth, the mortar "would suddenly tumble over on its side, and rolling out into the apartment it would set itself up and break into a gentle heel-and-toe polka," according to a *New York Times* article. "Warming up with the excitement its movements would quicken, and higher and higher it would bound until it reached the rafters overhead. Then it would remain passive sometimes for weeks and months together."

The mortar had originally been owned by a family that lived in one of the purportedly haunted houses. When that structure was torn down, parts of it were used in the construction of a new house. The owners of the new dwelling, having also acquired the mortar, would not allow it into their home. They kept it outside, perhaps in the belief that the mortar was somehow animated by the lignum vitae wood connected to the *Palatine*'s survivors.

Literally afraid to keep the mortar, its owners gave it to Block Island historian Samuel Truesdale Livermore in 1876. By 1882 Livermore had placed the artifact in Rhode Island Hall at Brown University in Providence, Rhode Island. The "dancing mortar," as it had come to be known, was still on view at Rhode Island Hall as late as 1959.

The legends of the Great Shippe, the *Dash,* and the *Palatine/ Princess Augusta* all inspired works by renowned nineteenth-century poets. Henry Wadsworth Longfellow, of "Song of

Hiawatha" and "The Midnight Ride of Paul Revere" fame, penned a thirteen-verse poem about the Great Shippe called "The Phantom Ship," from which these excerpts are drawn:

> A ship sailed from New Haven,
> And the keen and frosty airs,
> That filled her sails in parting
> Were heavy with good men's prayers.

. . .

> But Master Lamberton muttered,
> And under his breath said he,
> "This ship is so crank and waity
> I fear our grave she will be!"

> And the ships that came from England
> When the winter months were gone,
> Brought no tidings of this vessel!
> Nor of Master Lamberton.

. . .

> At last our prayers were answered:
> It was in the month of June
> An hour before sunset
> Of a windy afternoon.

When, steadily steering landward,
A ship was seen below,
And they knew it was Lamberton, Master,
Who sailed so long ago.

On she came with a cloud of canvas,
Right against the wind that blew,
Until the eyes could distinguish
The faces of the crew.

Then fell her straining top mast,
Hanging tangled in the shrouds,
And her sails were loosened and lifted,
And blown away like clouds.

And the masts, with all their rigging,
Fell slowly, one by one,
And the hulk dilated and vanished,
As a sea-mist in the sun!

In 1866 John Greenleaf Whittier wrote the eighteen-verse poem "The Dead Ship of Harpswell" about the dreaded repeated appearances of the spectral *Dash,* allegedly to escort a newly deceased relative of a crewman to the hereafter. In the last stanza Whittier suggests that the *Dash*'s visits were actually acts of compassion:

Let young eyes watch from Neck and Point,
And sea-worn elders pray,—
The ghost of what was once a ship
Is sailing up the bay.

. . .

For never comes the ship to port,
Howe'er the breeze may be;
Just when she nears the waiting shore
She drifts again to sea.

. . .

The dead-boat with the bearers four,
The mourners at her stern,—
And one shall go the silent way
Who shall no more return!

And men shall sigh, and women weep,
Whose dear ones pale and pine,
And sadly over sunset seas
Await the ghostly sign.

They know not that its sails are filled
By pity's tender breath,

> Nor see the Angel at the helm
> Who steers the Ship of Death!

Just a year later, Whittier published his controversial thirty-stanza poem about the *Palatine,* of which the following portion is the most relevant:

> Old wives spinning their webs of tow,
> Or rocking weirdly to and fro
> In and out of the peat's dull glow,
>
> And old men mending their nets of twine,
> Talk together of dream and sign,
> Talk of the lost ship Palatine,—
>
> The ship that, a hundred years before,
> Freighted deep with its goodly store,
> In the gales of the equinox went ashore.
>
> The eager islanders one by one
> Counted the shots of her signal gun,
> And heard the crash when she drove right on!
>
> Down swooped the wreckers, like birds of prey
> Tearing the heart of the ship away,
> And the dead had never a word to say.

And then, with ghastly shimmer and shine
Over the rocks and the seething brine,
They burned the wreck of the Palatine.

In their cruel hearts, as they homeward sped,
"The sea and the rocks are dumb," they said:
"There'll be no reckoning with the dead."

But the year went round, and when once more
Along their foam-white curves of shore
They heard the line-storm rave and roar,

Behold! again, with shimmer and shine,
Over the rocks and the seething brine,
The flaming wreck of the Palatine!

. . .

For still, on many a moonless night,
From Kingston Head and from Montauk light
The spectre kindles and burns in sight.

Now low and dim, now clear and higher,
Leaps up the terrible Ghost of Fire,
Then, slowly sinking, the flames expire.

And the wise Sound skippers, though skies be fine,
Reef their sails when they see the sign
Of the blazing wreck of the Palatine!

CHAPTER 8

COLONIAL "FLYER"

A marker affixed to a wall in the garden of Boston's Old North Church claims to commemorate two milestones in the history of human flight. One was the first nonstop airplane crossing of the United States. That twenty-seven-hour journey from Long Island to San Diego took place in 1923, the year the Massachusetts Society of the Colonial Dames of America placed the plaque at the Old North Church.

The other milestone, according to the plaque, occurred 166 years earlier, right at the Old North Church itself. "Here on September 13, 1757," the inscription reads, "John Childs who had given public notice of his intention to fly from the steeple of Dr. Cutler's church [Old North Church], performed it to the satisfaction of a great number of spectators."

Did a man actually fly from the 190-foot-tall spire of the Old North Church, in plain view of a multitude of witnesses, nearly 150 years before the Wright Brothers' first flight at Kitty Hawk, North Carolina? How did John Childs accomplish this incredible feat? And why has it remained hidden from the mainstream of history?

Literally everything known about John Childs and his achievement has been gleaned from short newspaper reports of his Boston demonstration. Childs introduced himself to "all Gentlemen and Ladies" of the town in an advertisement in an issue of the *Boston Gazette* newspaper. He claimed to be a man who "has flown off of most of the highest steeples in Old-England, and off of the Monument by the Duke of Cumberland's Desire." (The "Monument" was a 202-foot-tall stone column in London representing that city's recovery from the Great Fire of 1666, which destroyed three-quarters of its buildings. The Duke of Cumberland was the son of King George II of England.)

After presenting the public with this impressive résumé and claim of royal patronage, Childs then announced that he planned "this day, and two days following, to fly off of Dr. Cutler's Church, where he hopes to give full Satisfaction to all Spectators."

Childs had chosen the site of his demonstration with maximum visibility in mind. The Old North Church, built of brick in 1723, was then the tallest building in Boston. Even better from Childs's perspective, it stood atop one of the town's highest hills.

So far as his contemporaries were concerned, Childs made good on his promise. The *Boston Weekly News-Letter* newspaper reported that on September 13, 1757, Childs, "who had given

REPRINTED FROM *SKETCHES OF BOSTON, PAST AND PRESENT*, 1851. GODFREY MEMORIAL LIBRARY, MIDDLETOWN, CONNECTICUT

This is the Old North Church—but not the steeple—from which John Childs "flew" in 1757. The 190-foot spire that served as Childs's launching pad was destroyed by a storm in 1804. Its replacement, shown in this 1851 engraving, was fifteen feet shorter.

public Notice of his Intention to fly from the Steeple of Dr. Cutler's church, perform'd it to the Satisfaction of a great Number of Spectators."

The next day Childs, as announced, repeated his flight twice. He added some extra pizzazz to his third and final performance. According to the *Weekly News-Letter* report, Childs "set off with two pistols loaded, one of which he discharged in his descent, the other missing fire, he cock'd and snap'd again before he reached the place prepared to receive him."

Childs's flights captivated the public—so much so that, according to the *Weekly News-Letter*, they "led many People from their Business." To prevent any further frivolous distractions of the citizenry from their work, the *Weekly News-Letter* continued, Childs was "forbid flying anymore in the Town."

John Childs never again flew in Boston—or anywhere else in North America that historians have been able to find. But his three flights from the Old North Church's steeple had made news throughout the Northeast. Newspapers in New Hampshire, New York, and Pennsylvania picked up and reprinted the Boston journals' brief reports of his extraordinary feats.

Childs's three descents became part of Massachusetts lore. The Colonial Dames considered them significant enough to commemorate with their 1923 plaque. Childs even found his way into at least one modern chronology of aviation, which claimed that he used homemade wings to perform the "first successful heavier than air flight by a human being in America."

For more than 250 years, theories have been put forward to explain exactly what John Childs did on those September days in 1757. Did he leap from the spire of the Old North Church to soar with the assistance of some crude homemade glider or a pair of artificial wings? Did he jump off and float safely to earth by the use of a primitive type of parachute?

As it turns out, the information that enabled historians to determine what John Childs did that so enthralled colonial Bostonians is found in the very same *Weekly News-Letter* article that reported on his three demonstrations: "It is suppos'd from the Steeple to the Place where the rope was fix'd was about 700 feet upon a Slope, and that he was about 16 or 18 seconds performing it each time."

John Childs hadn't remained aloft by flapping fake wings or floating gently to the ground via some contraption. He had performed a stunt known as "rope flying," one that other men had carried out in England decades before Childs put on his show in Boston.

Historians Peter Benes and J. L. Bell have explained how Childs managed to "fly": One end of a rope was tied to the top of a tall structure—in this case the Old North Church steeple. The other end was fastened to the ground some distance away and drawn taut to create an angled tightrope.

The would-be "flyer" took a board and down its middle gouged a lengthwise groove through which the rope would run. Standing atop the steeple, Childs placed the board grooved-side down on the rope, so that it ran through the groove. He then lay chest-down on the board—like a child on a sled with runners, or a surfer paddling out into the water on a surfboard—and launched himself headfirst down the length of the rope.

As Childs hurtled forward, he used his arms and legs to maintain his balance. He had to keep the board from listing too far to one side or the other and dumping him off, which, depending on how high up he was when he fell, would have resulted in injury or possibly death. Holding a pistol in each hand and firing them off as he slid along the rope, as Childs did in his last demonstration, would have made this balancing act even more difficult, adding an extra element of risk to the stunt.

How did Childs manage to avoid breaking his neck when he literally reached the end of his rope? The secret to his safe landing was discovered in the memoirs of Samuel Breck, published posthumously in 1877. According to Breck, his mother had witnessed Childs's descent from the Old North Church steeple. She told her son that Childs slid along the rope until, in Breck's words, he "came safely to a pile of feather beds placed there to receive him."

An actual contemporary image of what John Childs likely did that day in Boston can be found in a work of art created a quarter of a century before he climbed to the top of the Old North Church's steeple. In 1733 the British artist William Hogarth painted *Southwark Fair,* depicting the amusements that occurred in that London neighborhood. In the background Hogarth included a man sliding headfirst along a rope that seems to be strung between two buildings—a rope flyer.

The facts of John Childs's early "flying" may be something of a letdown to generations who have seen astronauts travel safely to the moon and back. But to colonial Bostonians, it would have been a thrilling novelty. Using only a rope, a board, a bag of feathers, and his own coordination and courage, Childs had deliberately launched himself from a great height. He had not plummeted straight to the ground but instead had traveled through the air with some degree of control and come to a safe landing on terra firma. However briefly and imperfectly, John Childs had experienced the exhilaration of flying in a way that his earthbound spectators could only dream of.

CHAPTER 9

MEDIUM RISING

Connecticut and Massachusetts served as the unlikely stage for the opening acts of the career of one of the best-known spiritualists of the 1800s. In the space of just a few years in the mid-nineteenth century, southeastern Connecticut resident Daniel Dunglas Home emerged into the public eye as a medium who many believed had the ability to communicate with the dead and foretell the future, and in whose presence unseen spirits could cause heavy objects such as furniture to move—and even rise off the ground.

The story actually starts on the other side of the Atlantic, in Scotland. Daniel Dunglas Home, the third of eight children, was born in 1833 near the city of Edinburgh.

Home was a frail child from the start, and his upbringing was less than stable. When he was just a year old, an aunt and uncle who had no children of their own adopted him—even though both of Home's parents were still alive. Allegations that Home's father had a drinking problem and could be abusive toward his wife may have had something to do with the decision.

When Home was around nine years old, he emigrated from Scotland to the United States with his aunt and uncle. They settled near the town of Norwich in southeastern Connecticut. Home's parents and several siblings also eventually came to the same region of Connecticut. However, they took up residence in the town of Waterford, about a dozen miles from Norwich, and Home apparently never lived with them.

In his autobiography, *Incidents in My Life,* Home claimed that supernatural abilities ran in his family on his mother's side, going back at least three generations preceding Daniel Home. His mother, Home said, "had what is known in Scotland as the second sight." She "was a seer throughout her life," her son recalled, a gift that was either a blessing or a curse, depending on one's point of view. She possessed the ability to describe events that were taking place at a great distance and could predict the deaths of family members months in advance—including, ultimately, her own.

A couple of odd incidents occurred while Home was still quite young that could be considered evidence that he had inherited his mother's psychic talents. But the purported powers that would make him a celebrity among seers did not definitively manifest themselves until Home was thirteen.

Home and a friend had promised each other that whichever of them died first would try to contact the other from beyond the grave. One moonlit night, Home claimed he had a vision of the youth, who was more than 150 miles away and had been, so far as Home knew, in good health. Home, however, was certain that the vision heralded his friend's death. A few days later came confirmation that the boy had indeed died of a sudden illness at the time Home saw him in his vision.

Home's supernatural abilities increased, with new powers sometimes appearing unexpectedly, alarming Home as well as those around him. When Home's mother died sometime around 1849, he knew what had happened the moment it occurred, despite being miles away from her. Not long after losing his mother, Home began to hear rapping or knocking made by some unseen force on the walls of his bedroom in his aunt's house.

The morning after this phenomenon occurred, Home and his aunt, who had strongly conflicting views on religion, were getting ready to sit down to breakfast when, Home recalled, "our ears were assailed by a perfect shower of raps all over the table. I stopped almost terror-stricken to hear again such sounds coming with no visible cause."

The rapping sounds were significant in light of strange reports that had first begun coming out of Hydesville, New York, in 1848. Mysterious knockings suddenly began to be heard in the home of Margaret and John Fox and their two adolescent daughters, Margaret and Katie. It was quickly concluded that the rappings were caused by spirits seeking to contact the living, with Margaret and Katie being the focus of the phenomena.

News of this alleged extraordinary connection to the hereafter spread rapidly, attracting hundreds of people to the Fox home, where Margaret and Katie held séances in which the dead conveyed their messages by means of rapping. Many people believed that the Fox sisters had a direct line to the other side. Others were convinced that Satan was behind the knockings.

Home's aunt, who was familiar with the Fox sisters' story and sided with those who believed the rappings to be diabolical in origin, was terrified to hear them in her own home. "So you've brought the devil to my house, have you," she screamed at Daniel, who recalled that "in her uncontrollable anger, she seized a chair and threw it at me."

Next pieces of furniture began to move—without his aunt's assistance—when Home was present. The same thing happened when Home visited the residence of another aunt. There he claimed to have communicated for the first time with a spirit—that of his own mother, who assured him that "[y]ours is a glorious mission—you will convince the infidel, cure the sick, and console the weeping."

The aunt with whom Home lived at last couldn't stand the rappings and shifting furniture, never mind the hordes of people who, having heard about Daniel's strange abilities via word of mouth and newspaper reports, were coming to consult with him. Home was "turned out of house and home at the age of 18," he remembered, "and with three younger children dependent on me for support."

Home went to live temporarily with a friend in nearby Willimantic. The rappings, the furniture moving, and the contacts with the shades of the dead continued, attracting ever more attention. A newspaper report of a séance held in March 1851 included a participant's eyewitness account of how a heavy table "was moved without the Medium's hands or feet touching it at all. At our request, the table was turned over into our lap."

That story thrust Home—unwillingly, so he claimed—into the public eye like never before. He believed that his supernatural powers had been bestowed on him by God, and he felt a responsibility to use them in service to his fellow human beings. However, from that point on, he lamented, his life was not his own, as he was inundated with visits from people from all walks of life, including scientists, clergymen, and writers, for all manner of reasons—curiosity, scientific or theological inquiry, help in contacting a departed loved one. Home claimed complete ignorance of exactly how his supernatural powers operated, and he also contended that he had no control over them. Indeed, his abilities sometimes faded for extended periods of time but then eventually would return.

Home never charged a fee for his services as a medium. He did, however, accept donations and gifts, which ultimately provided him with a comfortable lifestyle.

Home soon moved from Willimantic to the neighboring town of Lebanon. The powers he displayed continued and even increased to include the ability to heal the sick.

For the next several years, Home moved around, to New Jersey, to New York City, to Springfield in Massachusetts, to Connecticut. His reputation grew, and people flocked from afar to wherever he happened to be in order to attend one of the séances he often held several times a day. He tried to study medicine, but his poor health made that impossible.

While Home allegedly could predict the future, talk to ghosts, receive messages via rappings, and even cure illness, it was the movement of furniture that seemed to most impress several of those who reported on his séances. It was something—tangible, for lack of a better word—that anyone in the room could witness.

The séance Home held on August 8, 1852, in South Manchester, Connecticut, involved a lot of impressive furniture shifting. But something new occurred that night, a milestone in Home's career as a medium.

The séance took place at the home of Ward Cheney, president of a manufacturing firm bearing his family's name that was well on its way to becoming the world's largest producer of silk fabric. Five men, including Cheney and Franklin Burr of Hartford, sat down at a table with Home. What ensued was reported by Franklin Burr two days later in the *Hartford Daily Times* newspaper, of which Burr's brother was editor.

The session began with Home's conveying messages from the spirit world to several men. Despite having been blindfolded, he was able to spell out the words by pointing to letters of the alphabet on a card. When there was some confusion over a particular word, enthusiastic rapping on the table would signal when the right guess had been made. A dramatic communication came across from two relatives of one of the men present, sailors whose ship had been lost at sea. Their message was accompanied by the tipping of the table as well as sounds like that of a ship caught in a gale—the flapping of sails, the creaking of the wooden vessel's boards. Suddenly, the table, which no one was touching, rose about a foot from the floor.

"A table weighing (I should judge) 100 pounds was lifted up a foot from the floor, the legs touching—nothing," Franklin Burr wrote. "I jumped upon it, and it came up again! It then commenced rocking without however allowing me to slide off, although it canted at least to an angle of 45 deg. Finally, an almost perpendicular inclination slid me off."

Another man took his turn leaping on the table in an attempt to subdue it, only to meet with the same result as Burr. "These things all happened in a room which was light enough to allow of our seeing under and over and all around the table, which was touched by no one, except the two persons who, respectively, got upon it to keep it down!" Burr continued.

But more was in store for the men gathered in Ward Cheney's home—something Daniel Home had never done before. Burr uttered a request "that the spirits would give us something that would satisfy every one in the room of their presence." He got a response.

A FEW WORDS ON AN UNPOPULAR SUBJECT.

To the Editor of the Hartford Times:

I wish to give a brief account of what I recently saw and felt in the presence of one of the media for the transmission of sounds, commonly known as "spiritual knockings" or communications. As the bare mention of this subject is apt to produce a whiff of impatient contempt among the majority of people (who apparently prefer derision to investigation), I will only allude, at this time, to a few occurrences which I would like to have explained either on Magnetic or "Odic" principles. I say this because it is *now* very generally conceded by *all* parties that many of the most singular of these manifestations are not produced by trickery. If this is the case (and few candid men at this day will deny it), it follows, as a corollary, that they must be explained by *one* of two things — either they are the strange product of some recondite principle of the human organism with which we have yet to form even the basis of an intelligent acquaintance; or, they are what they purport to be—the manifestations of an existence beyond the grave, of those we have known and loved on earth. Either they are

Suddenly, and without any expectation on the part of the company, the medium, Mr. Hume, was taken up in the air ! I had hold of his hand at the time, and I felt of his feet—they were lifted a foot from the floor ! He palpitated from head to foot with the contending emotions of joy and fear which choked his utterance. Again and again he was taken from the floor, and the third time he was carried to the lofty ceiling of the apartment, with which his hands and head came in gentle contact. I felt the distance from the soles of his boots to the floor and it was nearly three feet ! Others touched his feet to satisfy themselves.

This statement can be substantiated, if necessary.

I omitted to state that these latter demonstrations were made in response to a request of mine that the spirits would give us something that would satisfy every one in the room of their presence. The medium was much astonished, and more alarmed than any of the rest, who, I may add, took the matter calmly, though they were intensely interested.

The company present KNOW there was no *trickery* employed on this occasion. The question then is—*How* can Magnetism produce these manifestations ? To me the idea is more preposterous (and far less pleasant) than the spiritual solution of the matter.   F.

Franklin Burr gave the cautious title of "A Few Words on an Unpopular Subject" to the letter to the editor he signed only with the initial "F." In these excerpts of his letter he recounted his experience at a séance with medium Daniel Dunglas Home (spelled Hume, as that was how it was pronounced), for he was aware that it would likely be met by "a whiff of impatient contempt among the majority of people." But toward the end of his account published in the Hartford Daily Times *on August 10, 1852, Burr pulled no punches in describing his observation of what was claimed to be the first time Home ever levitated.*

"Suddenly, and without any expectation on the part of the company, the medium, Mr. Hume [*sic*], was taken up in the air!" Burr reported.

I had hold of his hand at the time, and I felt of his feet—they were lifted a foot from the floor! He palpitated from head to foot with the contending emotions of joy and fear which choked his utterance. Again and again he was taken from the floor, and the third time he was carried to the lofty ceiling of the apartment, with which his hands and head came in gentle contact. I felt the distance from the soles of his boots to the floor and it was nearly three feet! Others touched his feet to satisfy themselves.

Home himself seemed "much astonished, and more alarmed than any of the rest" of the men in the room, wrote Burr. It was the first—but by no means the last—time he had levitated.

"The company present *know* there was no *trickery* employed on this occasion," Burr claimed firmly in his report. However, he knew nonetheless that his account would be met with skepticism and possibly ridicule. His contribution to the *Hartford Daily Times* was titled "A Few Words on an Unpopular Subject," and Burr was not identified as the author.

Home's health, always precarious, worsened into what would ultimately be diagnosed as consumption, the nineteenth century's term for a lung ailment that was probably tuberculosis. His doctors recommended that the young man visit Europe to improve his health. He finally set sail for England in March 1855.

Home quickly became the supernatural toast of Europe. He was in demand for séances by everyone, including the royalty of various nations. He was particularly well known for his demonstrations of levitation, which he had first manifested in Connecticut.

Home never returned to the United States. But he apparently remained connected to the people who had known him in his earliest days as a seer. Ward Cheney, in whose house Home had astonished and frightened himself by rising to the ceiling, died in Connecticut in 1876. That same day, Daniel Home, five thousand miles away, on the other side of the Atlantic, sat down and wrote a letter to Cheney's daughter-in-law, consoling her on the death of her father-in-law.

Home himself died in Europe in 1886. A debate over whether he was a charlatan or a genuine seer had raged throughout his lifetime, and it continued after his death. Professional magicians have suggested methods Home might have used to perform many—but not all—of the phenomena that occurred during his séances. However, that he did employ such tricks has not been proven. More than a century after Daniel Dunglas Home's death, mystery still surrounds the life and abilities of the seer from New England.

CHAPTER 10

CAPTAIN KIDD'S TREASURE

For legendary buccaneer Captain William Kidd to have visited all—or even many—of the New England locations where lore reports he buried treasure during a single month in 1699, he would have needed a speedboat instead of a sailing ship. Various legends claim that Captain Kidd stashed loot at multiple spots along the thousands of miles of coastline from Maine's Casco Bay to Boston Harbor to Rhode Island's Block Island to southwestern Connecticut. One tale even claims that Kidd traveled more than one hundred miles inland to securely conceal valuables.

Whether his numerous far-flung buried treasures were genuine or not, Captain Kidd himself was a very real person. William Kidd was born sometime around 1650 in a town near the coast of Scotland. Left fatherless at the age of five, Kidd at some unknown time went to sea to make his livelihood.

By 1696 Captain Kidd had become a wealthy man, the result of decades of seafaring in the Caribbean. One of the lucrative activities in which he had been involved was privateering. This was the practice by which a government officially and openly commissioned privately owned vessels to attack and capture ships belonging to nations with which it was at war. Privateering allowed a nation to augment its naval power without expending any additional funds. The privateer's captain, crew, owners, and any investors were presented with an opportunity to get rich quickly, since they would receive a portion of the proceeds from the sale of any captured vessel and its contents.

Kidd's fortunes had also been enhanced by marriage to a rich widow half his age. He was a respected citizen of New York, where he made his home with his wife and young daughter in a three-story brick house on lower Manhattan. He had even paid for a pew in Trinity Church.

In 1696 a quartet of influential English noblemen, with the support of King William III himself, secretly retained Captain Kidd to perform a modified version of privateering. He was to seek out and capture pirate ships in the vast waters east of Africa and then sell their valuable cargoes and bring the proceeds back to England. He also had the authority to capture vessels affiliated with France, with which England was at war.

One-quarter of the profits from Kidd's expedition would be divided up among the crewmen. The king would receive 10 percent, and 15 percent would go to Kidd and a partner. The remaining 50 percent would be distributed among the investors in the scheme, which included not just the English lords but also other backers on both sides of the Atlantic.

Captain Kidd set sail from New York on his semi-clandestine mission on September 6, 1696. His ship, the *Adventure Galley,* was outfitted with thirty-two cannon. His orders were to carry out his mission and return within one year.

The *Adventure Galley* carried a crew of 150, many of whom were former pirates. Kidd had been able to recruit a crew—any crew—only by resorting to secretly promising them that they would divvy up 60 percent of the voyage's profits, rather than the one-quarter his backers had agreed to.

The *Adventure Galley* had barely vanished over the horizon before one of Kidd's New York investors wrote to London, telling what he knew of this new deal with the crew—which of course would slash Kidd's backers' take to a fraction of what had had been agreed upon. The informant suggested that the governors of all the English colonies on coastal North America and in the Caribbean be directed to seize Kidd and his ship should the privateer show up at one of their ports. An order to that effect was sent out before Kidd finally returned from his mission.

So Captain Kidd unknowingly had a cloud over his head from almost the very first. The mission on which he had embarked undoubtedly sounded like a grand idea when being discussed in the safety of London, but it proved impossible in practice. The seas were not crawling with pirate ships ripe for the boarding. In fact, perhaps only half a dozen such vessels were known to be active in the waters to which Kidd had been dispatched.

And even if Captain Kidd were to seize a pirate ship, that opened a can of worms that his backers either hadn't considered or wouldn't consider. What was to prevent the original owners of the pirates' stolen cargo from insisting on having their property returned to them, rather than being sold to benefit Kidd, his crew, and the backers? If Kidd kept the goods that he had taken from the pirates, didn't that make him—and any others who benefited from his action—in essence receivers of stolen goods, and little better than the pirates from whom he had seized the goods?

Kidd sailed around the southern tip of Africa, on a course that would ultimately take him to the waters of the Indian Ocean, the Arabian Sea, and the Red Sea. For the next three years, a run of bad luck—disease, problems with the ship, a ship-board uprising—and the occasional bad decision earned Kidd the (probably) unwarranted reputation of a pirate.

Early on in his mission, Kidd offended a Royal Navy commander, whom he suspected of wanting to force some of the *Adventure Galley*'s crewmen into the king's service. The naval officer decided that Kidd was in fact a pirate. Rumors to that effect spread, blackening Kidd's name. By July 1697 the malicious gossip was circulating in London itself.

At one point Kidd's crew staged a mutiny and proceeded to take actions that crossed the line into piracy. In January 1698 Kidd at last managed to capture a fat prize, the *Quedagh*

Merchant. The ship was sailing under a pass from France, with which England was at war.

The *Quedagh Merchant* proved to be carrying a valuable cargo of silk, opium, and jewels. However, it turned out that most of those goods belonged to a powerful figure in the Muslim world, a fact that touched off an ugly, complicated international incident.

Kidd's mishaps and mistakes had made him persona non grata to the English navy and English commercial interests in the region. He had also become a potential embarrassment—even a danger—to his secret financiers, who faced disgrace and possibly even death if it was discovered that they had backed the voyage that had touched off an international economic and political fiasco. Captain Kidd had become a pawn in a ruthless global contest of business and political forces—and pawns are often sacrificed to protect the more powerful pieces.

Captain Kidd returned to the Western Hemisphere in 1699—two years late in the eyes of his backers—determined to clear himself of the piracy accusations and to restore his honor. He brought with him much of the treasure that had been seized from the *Quedagh Merchant.* This included 75 pounds of gold, 150 pounds of silver, bales of Persian silk, and more than 70 jewels, including diamonds, emeralds, sapphires, and rubies—a fortune by anyone's definition.

Captain Kidd set sail from the Caribbean in a small ship with a crew of only a dozen men and headed for New York, his home port, where he had influential friends. By the beginning of June 1699, he had traveled as far north as the coast of Delaware. At that point he learned to his great consternation that some of the crewmen who had mutinied against him had already returned to the colonies. Kidd could count on their having spread slanderous tales about what he had been up to during his three-year absence—tales that almost certainly would have reached New York.

A cautious Captain Kidd lurked in the waters at the eastern end of Long Island Sound while he sought intelligence on what kind of welcome he could expect to receive in New York. Kidd dispatched a messenger to inquire of his lawyer in New York, a trusted colleague, which way the wind was blowing concerning the seafarer's reputation. He also asked the lawyer to let Mrs. Kidd know that her husband was back, alive and well.

The news that came back was not good. Kidd learned that he would be putting himself at risk of being arrested as a pirate if he sailed into the port he had left with such high hopes three years earlier.

Kidd next decided to test the political waters farther north. He sent his lawyer to Boston seeking information about what response awaited him should he go there to vindicate his reputation.

Once in Boston, Kidd's lawyer met with the governor of Massachusetts—who also happened to be one of the secret investors in Kidd's ill-fated voyage. The governor was a conniving, double-dealing man. For example, he had not yet revealed to anyone the fact that late in 1698 he had received a directive from London to arrest Captain Kidd on sight.

Kidd's lawyer returned with a verbal message of encouragement from the governor of Massachusetts, who suggested that Kidd sail to Boston. Kidd, by now thoroughly suspicious, sent a messenger back to Boston, asking that some assurances be put in writing and the documents sent to him.

Back from Boston came a letter written by the governor. He wrote that he had discussed Kidd's case with the King's Council. In the very carefully worded document, the governor said that in the council's opinion, "if your Case be so clear as you . . . have said, then you may safely come hither . . . and I make no Manner of Doubt but to obtain the King's Pardon for you. . . . I assure you, on my Word and honour, I will perform nicely what I have now promised."

The courier carrying the governor's letter found Kidd on Block Island, where he was waiting for his wife and daughter, whom he had not seen in three years. Kidd was enormously relieved by the governor's reassurances. He wrote back: "Upon receiving of your Lordship's letter, I am making the best of my Way for Boston."

Before doing so, however, Kidd, still cautious—or suspicious—sailed to Gardiner's Island off the eastern end of Long Island. There he actually did make arrangements to conceal some of his treasure. He gave the island's owner, John Gardiner, a chest filled with fifty pounds of gold and fifty pounds of silver

Treasure belonging to Captain William Kidd was indeed buried for safekeeping on Gardiner's Island off the eastern end of Long Island. However, Kidd himself did not personally supervise the process as depicted in this 1894 illustration by Howard Pyle. Kidd left the treasure with the owner of the island, John Gardiner, who decided underground was the most secure place for it. Kidd wasn't there when the treasure was dug up; in fact, he never saw it again.

to hold for him. Gardiner reportedly buried the chest to keep it safe until Kidd returned.

Kidd then set sail for Boston with his wife and their daughter. They arrived in Boston on July 1, 1699. Kidd spent the next week making his case before an increasingly uncooperative governor and council. Before a full week had passed, Kidd was arrested and confined to jail.

The Massachusetts governor learned that Kidd had entrusted considerable valuables to John Gardiner's keeping. In response to a summons from the governor, Gardiner brought the treasure Kidd had left with him to Boston. On March 10, 1700, those valuables were put on a ship that set sail for London. Also on board was Captain William Kidd, who, after eight months behind bars in Boston, was destined to be tried on charges of piracy and murder.

By now Kidd was an embarrassment and a liability to just about everyone who knew him. He was imprisoned for a year in London and finally was convicted in a two-day mockery of a trial. He was hanged on May 23, 1701.

Kidd's bad luck followed him even to the edge of eternity. When he was hanged, the rope broke. Superstition sometimes decreed that in such a case the condemned man's life should be spared. Kidd didn't receive the benefit of that doubt. He was hanged again, this time successfully.

Captain William Kidd was definitely dead. But he was not yet gone and certainly not forgotten—especially by those travelers who for years were greeted at the mouth of the Thames River by the sight of his rotting corpse suspended in a cage as a grisly warning against piracy.

Rumors began to circulate that Kidd had held back money and valuables from the authorities. Tales started to spring up about where Kidd might have concealed those riches. Anyplace Captain Kidd might conceivably have reached was considered a possible location for buried treasure—and many of those spots were in New England.

By the 1700s tales had emerged pinpointing Jewell Island in Maine's Casco Bay as the site of buried treasure, specifically Captain Kidd's fortune. When Kidd allegedly visited the island, he supposedly sent most of his crew off to secure a supply of fresh water. While they were away, Kidd and a couple of trusted men filled a copper kettle with treasure and buried it.

The discovery of what were purported to be directions to Captain Kidd's hidden treasure identified Conant's Island in Boston Harbor as the spot, according to an account by one Frederick T. Wallace, published in J. H. Temple's 1889 *History of the Town of Palmer, Massachusetts,* which is located in the south-central portion of that state. Early in 1849, so Wallace wrote, two cousins in their late teens were out chasing rabbits with a dog on the farm that belonged to Samuel Shaw, the father of one of the boys. The dog pursued a rabbit into a tight crevice in the rocks. The youths began pulling away stones, hoping to make the opening large enough either for the dog to enter or for one of them to reach in and grab the rabbit.

When one of the cousins extended his arm into the space in the rocks, he touched not the soft fur of a rabbit, but the smooth hardness of glass. He pulled out what proved to be a small bottle "hermetically sealed" by a lead stopper tightly wedged into the neck. The stopper was covered by a lead cap and secured by a wire, which sounds something like the way in which champagne is bottled. According to Wallace, the bottle was sealed, tellingly, "somewhat in the manner in which sea-faring persons prepared communications to be thrown overboard in time of distress, hoping the same may be washed upon some distant coast."

The excited cousins managed to unseal the bottle, but they weren't able to pull out the rolled-up document they could see inside. Impatient, they at last broke the bottle to get at the contents, which proved to be a letter supposedly written by Captain Kidd from his prison cell in Boston to a man named John Bailey in New York City.

In the letter Kidd asked Bailey to come to Boston to help him fight the accusations of piracy lodged against him. He then went on to write: "If I do not see you I will tell you where the money is. . . . It is buried on Conant's Island, in Boston Harbor, on the northwest corner of the island in two chests, containing from fifteen to twenty thousand pounds sterling, in money, jewels and diamonds. They are buried about four feet deep with a flat stone on them, and a pile of stones near by." The site, Kidd added, was about sixty rods (roughly a thousand feet) "up the side of the hill." Kidd and another man, since deceased, had hidden it when the crew was either asleep or abroad in Boston.

According to the letter, Kidd had already resorted to misinformation to protect his hidden treasure. Government officials "think I have got money buried down at Plymouth, or that way somewhere," Kidd confided. "They don't think it is so near Boston."

Kidd was revealing the location of his concealed wealth so that Bailey could retrieve it and use it to help Kidd bribe his way out of trouble. "It will buy a great many great people and all the poor I want in my favor," the letter stated.

That the letter ended up in a crevice in Palmer, well over a hundred miles from New York, left little doubt that it never reached John Bailey, and that Bailey never visited Conant's Island to follow the explicit directions to Kidd's buried treasure. The letter quite conveniently included information that could explain how it came to be concealed in such an unlikely spot.

Kidd informed Bailey that he had taken the precaution of entrusting delivery of the letter to a man who was illiterate and thus couldn't read it and go searching for the treasure himself. The bearer was to travel overland on the first leg of his journey from Boston to New York. "I told the man that brings this to you, if he met with any trouble or was taken by the Indians, to hide his papers in some safe place where he can find them if he got away. I will put them in the glass, for if he should get them wet or anything should happen to him they will be safe," Kidd's letter said.

That the Shaw cousins found the letter where they did suggests that Kidd's forebodings were justified. Something happened that caused the courier to follow Kidd's instructions and hide the bottle, and he was never able to return to recover it.

The bottle and the letter generated a sensation in the area around Palmer. So many people flocked to the Shaw farm to gaze upon them that the family, at last tired of the disruptive attention, consigned the artifacts to the safety of a bank vault.

The Shaw cousins embarked on their own personal treasure hunt later that same year. They joined the rush of fortune seekers in California, where gold had just been discovered. Before the youths embarked on their West Coast adventure, each made a sworn statement about his discovery of the bottle and letter and left it with his father.

"There can be no doubt of the genuineness of the Kidd letter," declared Frederick Wallace. Its authenticity was "undisputed and undoubted at the time by hundreds of gentlemen who visited the place and examined and read the paper." Wallace pointed out that no one in or anywhere near the small town of Palmer had the extensive knowledge of colonial history to compose such a convincing fake.

Jamestown, Rhode Island, is another location where Captain Kidd is rumored to have concealed treasure. This tale has at least some connection to documented fact. In June 1699, while waiting for his lawyer to return from his mission to the governor in Boston, Kidd sailed to Jamestown to see a retired seafaring buddy, Thomas Paine. While he was there, Kidd gave Paine several gold bars to hold for him.

Paine later told government investigators that he subsequently received a request for the gold from Mrs. Kidd, who was in Boston and desperately needed it to fund her attempts to win her husband's freedom from jail. Paine reported that he sent the gold to Mrs. Kidd. But lore claims that Kidd actually turned over much more treasure to Paine than just a few gold bars and that it may have been buried on Paine's land in Jamestown.

Block Island, where Kidd spent time while awaiting missives from Boston, is also reportedly the site of buried treasure. An article in the *New York Times* on October 19, 1884, reported that Kidd had buried treasure at Sandy Point.

What some believed was part of one of Kidd's buried treasures was accidentally found about two miles north of Bridgeport, Connecticut, according to an article in the February 16, 1884, issue of the *New York Times.* It reported that immigrant workers digging a bed for a new rail line had uncovered a carved powder horn with a silver tip that contained some English coins, a Spanish doubloon, and a scrap of parchment. Rumor said that even more had been discovered: silver objects, additional coins, sword hilts, and an iron box containing gold. The immigrants reportedly vanished, presumably with their newfound riches.

In their 1875 *History of the Town of Northfield, Massachusetts,* authors J. H. Temple and George Sheldon recounted the local legend that Captain Kidd and some of his men had transported a chest filled with gold up the Connecticut River to Clarke's Island in Northfield, where they buried the treasure. "Having placed the heavy chest in its hole," Temple and Sheldon wrote, Kidd's band "sacrificed by lot one of their number, and laid his body atop of the treasure, that his ghost might forever defend it from all fortune-seekers."

To go to the extraordinary lengths of hiding something on Clarke's Island demonstrates a level of caution—even paranoia—that was extreme even for wanted men hiding a valuable treasure. Clarke's Island is more than a hundred miles as the crow flies from the mouth of the Connecticut River. Even more daunting to any travelers would have been the river rapids at what today is the town of Enfield, Connecticut, only about halfway to Northfield. That patch of rough, shallow water prevented sailing vessels from proceeding any farther upriver until the nineteenth century, when a canal that allowed ships to bypass the rapids was built. For Kidd and his men to take the treasure to Northfield in the seventeenth century, they would have had to portage it around the rapids and then transport it the rest of the way either on a small sailing vessel or overland.

These are just a few of the countless legends and stories about where around New England Captain Kidd allegedly hid buried treasure. But there are also tales, sometimes involving the supernatural, about what happened to those who went in search of the hidden booty.

Here we once again pick up the story of Samuel Shaw of Palmer, Massachusetts. Later in 1849, he traveled to Boston to try to follow the detailed directions in the letter found on his property that purportedly led to a vast treasure hidden by Captain Kidd. Disappointingly, Shaw found that Conant's Island, now known as Governor's Island, had experienced major shoreline erosion. A century and a half of tide and waves had washed away the spot at which Kidd had supposedly buried the treasure. At that very moment, the government was building a seawall to prevent any more erosion.

To the bitterness of that disappointing revelation was added the acrimony of litigation. Samuel Shaw and his brother Gardner Shaw, whose sons had discovered the alleged Kidd letter, went to court over who should retain possession of the original document. The entire episode came to a disillusioning end when Samuel Shaw swore under oath that the letter was a forgery.

Many questions still remain. Why did Shaw believe that the letter was a fake? Was his son or his nephew aware of it? If it was a fraud, who perpetrated it, and why?

In hindsight, Samuel Shaw's revelation shouldn't come as a shock. In its precision and thoroughness, the Kidd letter would seem too good to be true. It explains everything with a comprehensiveness that centuries-old documents do only in historians' dreams.

The letter's directions to the treasure on Conant's Island are explicit. By including information that would have been of no interest or use to its intended recipient, the writer even conveniently offers an explanation as to how the message in a bottle came to be where it was found. All that would have mattered to John Bailey was that he had Kidd's letter in hand. Whatever instructions Kidd had given the messenger about what to do if he encountered trouble on the way to New York would have been of no value to Bailey—but it did nicely explain the highly improbable discovery of the message in Palmer.

Even one of the pieces of "internal evidence" Frederick Wallace had cited to support the "genuineness of the letter"—before Samuel Shaw's testimony debunked it—served to undermine the legitimacy of the document. The letter bore the date of "Boston, 1700–1." Before 1752 England and its colonies used two different calendars simultaneously: the Gregorian, in which the new year began on January 1, and the Julian, in which the new year did not begin until March 25. Thus, when a date between January 1 and March 25 was written, both the year into which that date fell under the Julian calendar (1700 in the case of the Kidd letter) and the year into which it fell under the Gregorian calendar (1701) were noted—as "1700–1." This "peculiar date," Wallace contended, made it clear that the letter had been written early in the eighteenth century.

However, Captain Kidd was held in jail in Boston from July 1699 to March 1700, at which point he sailed to London, never to return to North America. Any "double-dated" letter Kidd wrote from prison in Boston would have been written

"1699/1700." Kidd would have been in London, not Boston, when he wrote any letter dated 1700/01. Wallace may have known enough about the "double-dating" system to consider its use in the Kidd letter a sign of authenticity—but not enough about the timeline of Captain Kidd's life after July 1699 to realize that it was a revealing error.

Versions of a spine-tingling ghost story are told about what happened to people who tried to dig up Captain Kidd's treasure at sites that included Block Island, Clarke's Island in the Connecticut River, and Charles Island off Milford, Connecticut. An 1884 *New York Times* article reported in great detail the version told on Block Island.

The landlady of a hotel on the island recalled how, on a late autumn night, in the light of a full moon, her uncle and several friends went to the spot on Sandy Point where Kidd allegedly had buried his treasure. "It was understood that to be successful not a word must be spoken until the pot had been unearthed and removed," the reporter quoted the landlady.

After fifteen minutes of enthusiastic digging with shovels and pickaxes, the treasure seekers hit the literal jackpot—a large, rusty, heavy iron kettle. The men began scrabbling with their hands to clear away the remaining dirt and extract their discovery. At last they were just beginning to be able to lift it from the bottom of the hole when they spotted a boat offshore being rowed toward the beach. It carried a spectral contingent of seamen in old-fashioned dress, armed with flintlocks, with a man who could be none other than Captain Kidd in the bow, sword in hand.

"What most astonished the spell-bound group was that the boat and its occupants seemed to be of gray, impalpable mist," the storytelling landlady continued. "The phantom boat swept over the tumbling surf waves to the strand, the crew leaped on the shore, and in an instant a gray-white mist rushed up the slope, enveloping the hill and the money diggers. There was a vivid flash of lightning, followed by a peal of thunder."

The terrified treasure seekers had seen enough. They took to their heels. After they had put about five hundred yards between themselves and their work site, they paused to look back. The frightening apparition had vanished.

The men mustered their courage to return to the pit they had dug. Peering in, they saw nothing—no pot of gold, no depression left where they had sought to wrench it free. "Since then," the landlady declared, "no one has hunted for Kidd's treasure on Block Island."

That has undoubtedly not remained the case—neither for Block Island nor for the rest of New England. The idea of buried treasure waiting to be found, conferring instant riches on the discoverer, establishing a tangible connection with an exciting and romantic chapter of history, is just too tantalizing to resist. So long as people dream of such things, the legends of Captain Kidd's buried riches will continue to be told, and the treasures they speak of will still be sought.

CHAPTER 11

CHAMP

The Himalayas have the Yeti. Scotland has the Loch Ness Monster. The Pacific Northwest has Bigfoot. And New England has Champ. Champ is a massive, mysterious creature that some believe lives beneath the waters of Lake Champlain on the Vermont–New York border, surfacing just often enough to be spotted and keep its legend alive.

Reports of sightings of something strange in Lake Champlain began emerging in the 1860s, although for a time in the late twentieth century there was a widely circulated claim that the first documented sighting had actually been made all the way back in 1609. Even more intriguing was that this initial spotting of what was allegedly Champ had been made by none other than French explorer Samuel de Champlain, for whom the lake is named.

However, it turned out that Champlain's description of what he had observed in the lake had been significantly altered and exaggerated in the modern recounting. In actuality, Champlain

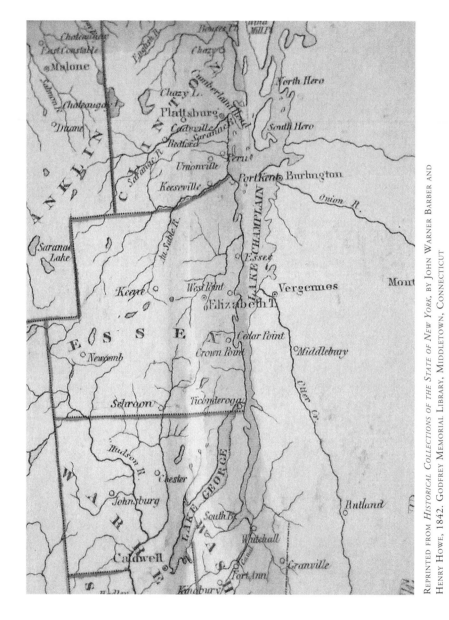

Reprinted from *Historical Collections of the State of New York*, by John Warner Barber and Henry Howe, 1842. Godfrey Memorial Library, Middletown, Connecticut

A nineteenth-century map shows Lake Champlain, the stomping— or more accurately, splashing—grounds of the crafty creature (some say cryptid) known as Champ.

wrote of seeing a fish that the local Native Americans said could reach ten feet in length. The one Champlain had personally observed, while not nearly that long, had been, the explorer wrote, "as big as my thigh, and had a head as large as my two fists, with a snout two feet and a half long, and a double row of very sharp, dangerous teeth." Even more impressive, Champlain wrote, the animal's body was "protected by scales of a silvery gray colour and so strong that a dagger could not pierce them."

Clearly, Champlain had gotten a look at one seriously scary fish, of a species he had never before seen. But he obviously didn't consider it any kind of mysterious monster.

It would be more than two centuries before a sighting of a bizarre creature in Lake Champlain would find its way into print. That report appeared in the July 24, 1819, issue of the *Plattsburgh Republican* newspaper, published in Plattsburgh, New York, which is located at approximately the midpoint on Lake Champlain's north-south shoreline. The heading of the item, which was identified as a communication to the publisher of the *Republican,* referred to the "Serpent on Lake Champlain."

According to the item, "On Thursday last, the inhabitants on the shore of *Bulwaggy* [Bulwagga] *Bay,* were alarmed by the appearance of a monster, which from the description may be a relation of the *Great Sea Serpent.*" Around eight o'clock in the morning, one "Capt. Crum" saw

at the distance of not more than two hundred yards, an unusual undulation of the surface of the water, which was followed by the appearance of a monster rearing its head more than fifteen feet and moving with the utmost velocity to the south—at the same time lashing with its *Tail* two large Sturgeon and a Bill-fish which appeared to be engaged in pursuit.

So far this sounds similar to later accounts of Champ sightings. However, the next two sentences begin to raise some doubts. "After the consternation occasioned by such a terrible spectacle had subsided," the *Plattsburgh Republican* reported,

Capt. Crum took a particular survey of this spectacular animal, which he describes to be about 187 feet long, its head flat with three teeth, two in the under and one in the upper jaw, in shape similar to the sea-horse—the color black, white star in the forehead and a belt of red around the neck—its body about the size of a hogshead [a wooden barrel large enough to contain more than a thousand pounds of something] with bunches on the back as large as a common potash barrel [a wooden container thirty inches tall]—the eyes large and the color of a pealed onion. He continued to move with astonishing rapidity towards the shore for about a minute, when suddenly he darted under water and has not since been seen.

Captain Crum must have possessed extraordinary powers of self-control and observation to have taken in so much detail about a startling creature that was visible for not much more than a minute, in motion, and six hundred feet away. And this animal—black, with a white star on its forehead and a red stripe around its neck—is perhaps the most flamboyant variation on Champ ever described.

"Many fishing boats have been on the look out [*sic*]" for the creature, the author of the *Plattsburgh Republican* communication continued. "Capt. Crum informs me that he has sent an express to Capt. Rich of Boston, communicating this intelligence, but is fearful that before his arrival the disturber of our waters may be chased to a pickerel."

The communication was signed "Horse Mackerel." Such a signature would seem to be a dead giveaway that this report was more likely a spoof than a sincere sighting. But the item can't be entirely discounted. Contributors to newspapers in the early nineteenth century sometimes hid their identity with unusual pseudonyms—although they were usually writing about serious topics like politics, not supernatural sightings. In 1820 a man named William Crumb was in fact living about thirty miles from the location referred to in the article (although whether he was a captain has yet to be determined). And four men with the last name of Rich were living in Boston that same year (again, their status as captains has yet to be established).

Once stories of sightings in Lake Champlain began to spread in the 1860s, it didn't take long for a high-profile huckster to try to take advantage of the sensational reports. Entertainment entrepreneur extraordinaire P. T. Barnum—himself by now a living legend—offered a hefty cash reward to anyone who caught and delivered to him—dead or alive—one of whatever it was that was startling people in Lake Champlain.

In the past 150 years, more than three hundred sightings of some kind of outlandish creature in Lake Champlain have been reported. A sign in Port Henry, New York, which proclaims itself the "Home of Champ," keeps track of purported Champ sightings that have occurred over the past century in Bulwagga Bay (at the southernmost end of the lake) alone. The list numbers more than one hundred, and it continues to grow.

Champ appeared not to favor any one location over the decades, having been seen at numerous spots around the lake. People have reported sighting an unidentified swimming object from positions on the New York, Vermont, and Quebec shores of Lake Champlain. Passengers on nineteenth-century steamboats and twentieth-century ferries plying the waters of the lake have claimed to see an unidentifiable, inexplicable creature—and sometimes dozens of people have claimed to see it at the same time.

Witnesses' descriptions have varied widely. There is, of course, Captain Crum's 1819 report of the 187-foot-long, three-toothed creature. In 1883 a New York county sheriff named Nathan Mooney reported that while standing on the shore of Lake Champlain, he saw what he called a "gigantic water serpent" about 150 feet out into the water. Sheriff Mooney estimated that the creature was only a fraction as large as the one described in 1819—a mere thirty feet long.

Other accounts have estimated the creature to be no longer than ten feet. Its color has been reported as running the gamut from white to green to reddish brown. One account even said that it had white spots inside its mouth! Witnesses have likened the creature to a snake, have spoken of its having a long and flexible neck, have said it resembled a dinosaur, or reported that it had several undulating humps, almost like the classic image of a Chinese dragon.

A major event in the ongoing debate over the existence of the reclusive aquatic animal occurred in 1977. On July 5 of that year, a tourist from Connecticut snapped a still photograph that appears to show the top of a creature's humped back just breaking the surface. It has a long, thick serpentine neck and head protruding from the water, seeming to face away from shore.

The photographer estimated that the—whatever it was—was about 150 feet from where she was standing on the shore when she took the shot. She estimated the neck to be about six feet long, and the entire animal to be between twelve and fifteen feet long. This sighting was more than a quick glimpse; the creature remained in view above the lake's surface for at least four minutes.

The photograph wasn't made public until four years later. It created a tremendous stir, appearing in *Time* magazine and the *New York Times,* among other publications.

By 1982 Champ had become such a New England celebrity that the Vermont House of Representatives passed a resolution officially protecting the creature "from any willful act resulting in death, injury or harassment." New York State legislators soon followed suit. But what was it that the politicians had protected?

Some people believe that what is seen in the 1977 Connecticut tourist's photograph, and what people have been claiming to observe in Lake Champlain for generations, is a "cryptid." This is an animal erroneously thought to be extinct.

The most famous example of a cryptid is a fish known as the coelacanth. That such an animal once existed was known from the many fossils that have been discovered. However, the coelacanth was generally believed to have been extinct for more than sixty million years.

That scientific assessment was proven wrong in 1938, when a coelacanth turned up in the haul of a boat that had been fishing in the waters off the coast of South Africa. Both that specimen and several others discovered over the next few decades were dead by the time they were identified. A couple of still-living coelacanths have survived for less than a day after being caught, long enough for scientists to examine them.

Within just the last two decades, photographs and video footage have been taken of living coelacanths swimming in their natural environment, at least six hundred feet beneath the surface of the ocean. The fish, which are classified as a critically endangered species, are six feet long and weigh around 175 pounds.

So, if the coelacanth managed to survive undetected for tens of millions of years, why, it has been argued, couldn't the same type of phenomenon have occurred in Lake Champlain? The lake has existed as a distinct body of water for ten thousand years. It is 120 miles long, 400 feet deep at spots, and covers an area of 435 square miles. It may not be the ocean, but the lake is still large enough for an extremely shy survivor of a prehistoric era—or generations of survivors, since no single such animal could live for ten millennia—to hide in.

There are many theories about what type of a cryptid Champ might be. It has been suggested that Champ is descended from a dinosaur that somehow survived whatever global disaster wiped out all the others of its kind. Another theory posits that Champ might be a longer, leaner prehistoric version of a whale. Several people have conjectured that Champ is related to the plesiosaur, an aquatic reptile that disappeared from the earth sixty-five million years ago. The plesiosaur had a long, flexible neck and large flippers, which seem to fit some descriptions of Champ.

Champ has always piqued the fascination of lovers of the unknown and the unexplained. But the allegations about an unidentified creature in Lake Champlain have also attracted serious scrutiny by scientific investigators. The 1977 tourist's photograph that caused such a sensation was analyzed by experts at the

University of Arizona and the University of British Columbia, with inconclusive results in both cases.

In 2002 Benjamin Radford and Joe Nickell conducted a study of the Champ phenomenon for the Committee for Skeptical Inquiry, and their findings were presented in the July 2003 issue of the group's publication, the *Skeptical Inquirer*. They interviewed residents in the Lake Champlain area, had the 1977 photograph analyzed, and used sonar to search for evidence in the lake. They concluded that there is "not a single piece of convincing evidence for Champ's existence."

That assessment didn't put a dent in Champ's popularity or in the continuing pursuit of evidence. Expensive expeditions have been launched to scour Lake Champlain for any sign of what may be living deep in its waters. Advanced technology such as echolocation has detected sounds beneath the surface of the lake that resemble those emitted by dolphins or whales. But those are sea creatures that couldn't possibly survive in the fresh water of Lake Champlain.

In recent decades Champ has been the topic of several books for adults and children alike, and at least one formal conference. Television documentaries have recounted the story for international audiences. Groups have been formed, and Internet sites have been established to record Champ's history and keep abreast of new findings.

Sightings, including one caught on videotape in 2005, continue to be reported. In the summer of 2008, a dozen enthusiasts conducted a Champ Expedition that failed to turn up any new information. Another one was reportedly being planned for 2009.

What are some of the more prosaic explanations for reports by hundreds of people who were certain they had seen *something* exceedingly strange in Lake Champlain? It has been conjectured that, just as Samuel de Champlain was astounded by the huge fish he saw four centuries ago, some modern witnesses may also have observed such known inhabitants of Lake Champlain and mistaken them for a mysterious creature or monster. Candidates for these deceptive fish include the gar and the sturgeon, the latter of which can grow, in extreme cases, as long as twelve feet.

Schools of fish or a string of playful otters emerging from the water at intervals as they play a watery game of "follow the leader" might also account for some sightings. So could large logs bobbing to the surface, propelled by the pressure from gases produced by the process of decay.

Elusive, mysterious, called a fake by some and a scientific wonder by others, Champ has proven an economic boon for the Lake Champlain region. Port Henry, New York, site of the sign that chronicles Champ sightings, sponsors an annual "Champ Day" celebration, complete with a parade featuring floats with fanciful depictions of the creature. Every kind of souvenir imaginable—from the ubiquitous T-shirt to key chains to mugs—bearing some artist's rendition of the "likeness" of Champ is sold. No one can say for sure how many people visit

Lake Champlain hoping to catch a glimpse of the mysterious creature that purportedly resides in its waters.

Champ may be something left over from prehistoric days, an animal that simply hasn't been discovered yet, a case of mass wishful thinking, misinterpreted natural phenomena, a hoax—or something else entirely. The only evidence that could answer that riddle once and for all would be the capture of a live specimen, or the discovery of a dead one, as happened in the case of the coelacanth. What is indisputable is that the extraordinary amount of time, energy, and expertise that has been lavished on Champ is testimony to the power of legends, and the irresistibility of mysteries.

CHAPTER 12

THE CHARTER OAK

You may have heard of the Charter Oak," wrote the special travel correspondent who used the pen name of Mark Twain in the March 3, 1868, issue of San Francisco's *Alta California* newspaper. "It used to stand in Hartford. The Charter of the State of Connecticut was once hidden in it, at a time of great political tribulation, and this happy accident made it famous."

After surviving for more than a millennium, the Charter Oak had fallen barely a dozen years before Twain's visit to Hartford, toppled by a windstorm in 1856. "Anything that is made of its wood is deeply venerated by the inhabitants and is regarded as very precious," Twain told his readers. He went on to describe his tour of Hartford with one of the city's residents.

> He showed me a beautiful carved chair in the Senate Chamber. . . . "Made from Charter Oak," he said. I gazed upon it with inexpressible solicitude. He showed me another carved chair in the House. "Charter Oak,"

he said. I gazed again with interest. Then we looked at the rusty, stained and famous old Charter, and presently I turned to move away. But he solemnly drew me back and pointed to the frame. "Charter Oak," said he. I worshipped.

Twain's guide next ushered him down the street to the Wadsworth Atheneum, the first public art museum in the United States, which boasted a fine collection of paintings. "I wanted to look at the pictures," Twain said, but his guide thwarted him.

[Instead he] conveyed me silently to a corner and pointed to a log, rudely shaped somewhat like a chair, and whispered "Charter Oak." I exhibited the accustomed reverence. He showed me a walking stick, a needlecase, a dog-collar, a three-legged stool, a boot-jack, a dinner-table, a ten-pin alley, a tooth-pick.

Twain tried to divert the man from his obsessive determination to show the author every item fashioned of wood from the historic tree with the wry suggestion, "[N]ow let us go and see some Charter Oak, for a change." Unfortunately, the ploy backfired. "I meant that for a joke," Twain reported. "But how was he to know that, being a stranger? He took me around and showed me Charter Oak enough to build a plank road from here to Great Salt Lake City."

Twain's account of being subjected to Charter Oak overexposure is amusing—and probably not all that much of an exaggeration. But it was unfortunate that excessive Victorian-era sentimentality and ancestor worship caused Connecticut residents to rhapsodize to an absurd degree over any stump or splinter of the tree. For the legend that spawned this reverence had its origins in a very real story of how Connecticut colonists had dared to stand up to the tyranny of an English king nearly a century before the American Revolution.

The tale has its roots in the 1630s, when groups of Puritans left the Massachusetts Bay Colony to establish three separate settlements in what was then wilderness on the western bank of the Connecticut River, approximately twenty-five miles from Long Island Sound. In 1639 those three settlements—Wethersfield, Windsor, and Hartford—organized themselves under a framework of government called the Fundamental Orders. Thus was born the Colony of Connecticut.

For the next two decades, the Connecticut Colony governed itself and expanded geographically up and down the Connecticut River and to the east and west as well. The English government on the other side of the Atlantic paid little attention to what was occurring on the North American frontier. Beginning in the 1630s, England was embroiled in a civil war that led to the beheading of King Charles I in 1649. For the next ten years, England was governed primarily by Puritans, whose leaders had no inclination to meddle with their coreligionists in New England.

But that all changed with the news that Puritan rule had not long survived the death of Lord Protector Oliver

Cromwell in 1658. In 1660 the son of the beheaded King Charles I returned from exile and ascended to the throne as King Charles II.

Suddenly, Connecticut Colony officials were confronted with a most inconvenient fact. They had no legal authority to be governing themselves under the Fundamental Orders, as they had been doing for more than a generation. In fact, if this logic were taken to the extreme, it might be decided that they had no legal right even to be where they were. The new English monarch could very well decide that they were nothing more than squatters, subject to eviction.

Bold and swift action was essential to assure the colony's survival. To that end, Connecticut governor John Winthrop Jr. sailed for London, where he hoped to negotiate some sort of resolution with the new king and his advisers.

Winthrop proved to be an outstanding negotiator. In 1662 he managed to secure from King Charles II a royal charter that didn't simply legitimize the Connecticut Colony's existence. The document also granted Connecticut a degree of self-government so extraordinarily extensive and liberal that the colony was all but independent of English control.

The royal charter provided for a governor, a lieutenant governor, and a legislature—all to be elected by the voters of Connecticut. The only significant restraint was the requirement that the Connecticut legislature not pass any laws that conflicted with those of England.

The charter even came with a special added bonus. For more than two decades, the New Haven Colony had existed independently of the Connecticut Colony to its north. Under the charter's provisions, the New Haven Colony was absorbed—against its will—into the Connecticut Colony.

The royal charter—a magnificent vellum document several feet in length, embellished with a prominent portrait of a bewigged King Charles II—arrived in Hartford, and once again, life was good in the halls of Connecticut government. So it remained for another quarter century, until King Charles II died in 1685.

Charles II was succeeded on the throne by his brother, James II—who soon hit not just Connecticut but all of New England with a nasty surprise. King James II didn't share his late brother's hands-off attitude toward England's North American colonies.

Shortly after ascending the throne, the new monarch set in motion a process to combine New York, Rhode Island, Massachusetts Bay, Plymouth, New Jersey, and Connecticut into a single mega-colony, the Dominion of New England, thus more firmly asserting his control over all of them. The new entity would be ruled over by King James's hand-picked governor, Sir Edmund Andros, who would have his headquarters in Boston.

However, creating the Dominion of New England would require rescinding charters previously granted to several of the affected colonies—Connecticut included. For nearly two years

Connecticut officials managed to evade complying with a series of royal letters and directives and to avoid being forced into the Dominion.

Governor Andros finally became fed up with Connecticut's refusal to cooperate. In late October 1687 Andros alerted colonial officials in Hartford that he would be visiting them. He was coming for the purpose of formally folding Connecticut into the Dominion—and to take back the royal charter. Connecticut's leaders had but a few days to decide on a course of action.

Andros arrived in Hartford on October 31, 1687, and he brought some serious backup: seventy armed and mounted soldiers. After Andros pointedly settled himself into the governor's chair, the royal commission authorizing him to rule over the Dominion of New England was read publicly. Next was read the king's directive to make Connecticut part of the Dominion.

This much of the story is documented history. The events that allegedly occurred during the next forty-eight hours are what gave birth to the legend of the Charter Oak.

On November 1, Connecticut governor Robert Treat and other members of the colony's government met with Andros and his entourage, probably in a room in a local tavern. Connecticut leaders staged what amounted to a colonial version of a filibuster. They discussed and debated with Andros, buying time. The sun went down, the room grew dark, and candles were lit.

Their arguments at last exhausted, Connecticut officials reluctantly placed the royal charter on a table. But before

Governor Andros could lay his hands on the document, legend says that the room was plunged into total darkness.

How that was accomplished, tradition does not explain. Perhaps a Connecticut official feigned illness and collapsed on the table, knocking over the candles and extinguishing them. Or maybe some coordinated "clumsiness" on the part of a couple of men led to the same result. However it happened, legend says that when the candles were once more lit, the charter had vanished.

During the brief period of darkness, legend continues, someone had grabbed the precious parchment and handed it out a window to a waiting man, who ran off into the night with it. But where in a tiny colonial town do you hide an enormous roll of vellum so securely that a search by seventy men won't turn it up? The solution, so the story goes, was to conceal the charter in a large cavity in an enormous ancient oak tree.

History doesn't record Governor Andros's reaction, or whether he launched any kind of search for the missing document. Whether Connecticut officials snatched the charter and stashed it in the hollow of an oak tree, or employed some other method, it is known for certain that Sir Edmund Andros left Hartford without the document he had ridden perhaps a hundred miles to retrieve.

However frustrating his failure to secure the charter may have been—especially if it was kept from him through the use of subterfuge—it mattered not at all to Andros's achievement of his primary goal. After twenty-five years of existence, the book was closed—literally—on the system of government authorized by the royal charter of 1662. Connecticut ceased to exist as a separate colony, to become just one more component of the Dominion of New England.

For eighteen months Connecticut endured the irritation of Sir Edmund Andros's autocratic rule. Then, in 1689, news reached Boston that King James II had been driven from his throne and replaced by the more reasonable King William and Queen Mary. Bostonians wasted no time slapping Andros and his cohorts behind bars, and the Dominion of New England was no more.

When word of King James's ouster and Edmund Andros's imprisonment was received in Hartford, Connecticut's royal charter was brought forth, and the electorate voted to resume governing the colony under its provisions. However, the fact that government under the charter had been suspended during the year and a half of Connecticut's forced incorporation into the Dominion of New England continued to cast a lingering, unsettling shadow.

Finally, in 1693, Connecticut dispatched Fitz-John Winthrop, son of Governor John Winthrop Jr., to London to persuade King William and Queen Mary to reaffirm the legitimacy of the document that Governor Winthrop had obtained more than thirty years earlier. One of the points put forward to support the continuing legitimacy and authority of the royal charter was the fact that the actual document had never been relinquished to the king's representative.

After four years Fitz-John Winthrop accomplished his mission. The royal charter of 1662 was sanctioned to continue to serve as the framework of Connecticut's government. It remained in effect until well after the American Revolution. The charter was finally replaced in 1818 by a constitution written by a convention of representatives from each town.

The story that the royal charter had been hidden in a massive oak tree to keep it out of the hands of the king's emissary began to appear in print in the late 1700s. The majestic tree—with a trunk seven feet in diameter, of an age reputed to be a thousand years—that had allegedly been a safe haven for the charter became a cherished symbol of Connecticut's commitment to liberty and independence, as well as its determination to defy anyone who tried to take them away.

By the 1830s the Charter Oak had been enshrined in Connecticut lore. Its story was published in books, it was hailed in poetry and song, and it was selected as the subject for some of the earliest photographs ever taken in Connecticut. When an anti-slavery newspaper began publication in Hartford, it was named, naturally, the *Charter Oak*.

When the ancient giant at last was toppled by a summer windstorm in 1856, Hartford mourned as if a dear family member had died. Firearms magnate Sam Colt sent a band over from his armory to play dirges for the fallen tree, and it was

THE CHARTER OAK.

Lith. of D.W. Kellogg & Co Hartford, Ct

By the 1830s, the massive, gnarled, ancient Charter Oak had become a venerated icon of Connecticut history, depicted in illustrations in books and lithographs.

photographed for posterity. Paintings captured its stature and majesty. Poetry paid tribute to it.

However, unlike the respectful treatment that would be accorded a human body, the Charter Oak's "corpse" was instantly subjected to a feeding frenzy. Everyone, it appeared, wanted a piece of the historic tree. In addition to the objects Mark Twain saw, wood from the Charter Oak was carved into an almost countless array of objects, such as pianos, chess sets, goblets, crucifixes, miniature furniture, a gavel, a cradle for Sam Colt's son, snuffboxes, and jewelry, including rings, earrings, bracelets, and hideously clunky brooches featuring oak leaf and acorn motifs.

"It is a shame to confess it," Twain wrote in his 1868 *Alta California* article, "but I did begin to get a little weary of Charter Oak." The people of Connecticut, however, were of a very different mind, about both the tree as a symbol and its physical remains, an attitude that has persisted to this day.

In 1907 the Society of Colonial Wars in the State of Connecticut erected a large stone monument to mark the site where the Charter Oak once stood. That monument still stands, wedged among the residences, stores, businesses, and streets of an urban neighborhood about as far removed as could be imagined from the frontier landscape that was Hartford in 1687.

"Charter Oak" has been incorporated into the names of everything from an insurance company to a credit union to a bridge to state government programs. It has been used to market bus lines and lawn mowers and hard liquor. When Connecticut instituted a lottery in 1972, the logo was a silhouette of the Charter Oak, with dollar signs in place of the leaves. When former Republican U.S. senator Lowell Weicker formed a third political party as the basis for his successful run for the governorship of Connecticut in 1990, he called it simply "A Connecticut Party" and used the Charter Oak as its logo. Connecticut's entrant in the series of state quarters issued by the U.S. Mint features a single image: the Charter Oak.

The Charter Oak literally lives on in first-generation "descendants"—trees sprouted from acorns harvested from the historic oak itself—that grow on the Connecticut State Capitol grounds and in adjacent Bushnell Park. In 2000 the Connecticut Department of Environmental Protection celebrated Arbor Day by distributing second-generation Charter Oak descendant seedlings—grown from acorns harvested from those first-generation descendants—to towns across the state.

The Senate Chamber chair carved from the Charter Oak upon which Twain looked with "inexpressible solicitude"—a five-foot-tall, heavily carved piece of furniture that, ironically, vaguely resembles a medieval throne—can still be seen by visitors today, in the Connecticut State Capitol. And the unfurled royal charter of 1662, still encased in the Charter Oak frame that Twain politely "worshipped" back in 1868, is on view at the Museum of Connecticut History in the Connecticut State Library in Hartford.

CHAPTER 13

HIDDEN IN THE WALLS

Unsuspected by their current occupants, hundreds of historic New England houses are hiding inside their walls objects purposely concealed there by previous owners. These secret stashes are usually discovered only in the course of renovation work. They do not, alas, consist of chests of valuable coins, or silver teapots, or rare jewels, but of shoes—old, worn-out shoes.

Shoes have been found in the walls—as well as under the floors, in the roofs, and in the chimneys and staircases—of old houses throughout New England. Countless shoes have undoubtedly been uncovered over the centuries. But they tended to inspire little more than passing curiosity on the part of the person who found them before they were tossed away with the other debris left over from tearing into walls. Not until the mid-twentieth century did these puzzling discoveries begin to attract the attention of scholars.

The best-documented examples of hidden shoes tend to be ones found in the walls of houses belonging to preservation or historical organizations that are taking pains to keep a detailed record of everything that occurs during a renovation project. Private homeowners have also begun to recognize that there is something significant about the worn-out footwear they come across unexpectedly during their remodeling, and sometimes they report their discovery to the local historical society.

Curiously, only one shoe of a pair will typically be found. When two or more are discovered, they usually don't match each other. Children's footwear is most frequently uncovered. Sometimes a cache of shoes of varying sizes turns up. In such cases, it has been theorized that one shoe from each member of a family was included.

The Ward-Heitman House in West Haven, Connecticut, is a historic house museum dating to 1725. During recent restoration work, a single shoe was found under the floor of an upstairs room. At Sycamores, a house built in 1788 and owned by the South Hadley Historical Society in Massachusetts, renovators were taking down part of an ell that had been added sometime after the original construction. Between the exterior and interior walls, they discovered three ancient shoes.

A jackpot of hidden objects was discovered during recent restoration work at the Hancock-Clarke House in Lexington, Massachusetts. It was here that rebel leaders Sam Adams and John Hancock were staying when British soldiers looking to arrest them had a fateful meeting with Minutemen on Lexington Green in April 1775 that ignited the American Revolution. The

THE *LEXINGTON MINUTEMAN* NEWSPAPER

When workers restoring the Hancock-Clarke House in Lexington, Massachusetts, opened one wall, they discovered hidden inside half a dozen worn-out shoes from the 1700s—evidence that one generation's trash is an earlier generation's talisman.

Hancock-Clarke House cache included six shoes from the 1700s, a box to hold musket cartridges, a shoe buckle, a letter—and, bizarrely, a child's corset!

New Englanders apparently brought this peculiar practice with them from the Old World. In England, shoes dating back to the medieval era have been discovered in walls.

But why go to the trouble of concealing something that not even the most desperate thief would want to steal, in a place where it would be inaccessible without tearing out a wall, which indicates there was no intention of retrieving it at a later time?

Not surprisingly, no one has yet been able to explain such seemingly illogical behavior with any certainty.

Cultural historians, however, have put forward several theories. Some have conjectured that the practice is rooted in the ancient custom of sacrificing a person and placing the body in the foundation of a new building. This grisly ritual was performed presumably to gain the favor of some pagan deity to secure the structure's soundness, or to protect it from evil spirits. The shoes are most commonly found hidden in walls near doors or windows or fireplaces—openings through which (or so it was believed) malevolent spirits would have the easiest access to a structure. Another theory holds that putting a shoe in the wall guaranteed that its owner would always find his way back home.

But why shoes? Why not stockings, or hats, or shirts? Again, the reason is a mystery, although theories abound. Most shoes were made of leather, which is the tanned hide of a dead animal. When human or even animal sacrifice became taboo as a pagan practice, perhaps leather was deemed the next closest thing available. For centuries, shoes have symbolized good luck and fertility (which explains why they are often tied to the back bumper of newlyweds' cars).

And why old shoes? Once more, no one knows for sure, but some have made educated guesses. Before the establishment of mass production in the mid-1800s, shoes were made by hand and thus were special and very expensive. They were worn as long as possible, repaired and patched repeatedly, until they literally began to fall apart. Penny-pinching Yankees likely would have cringed at the thought of walling up a new shoe. Beyond the issue of thriftiness, years of wear would mold a leather shoe to the shape of the wearer's foot, making it unique to that person.

Shoes are the most common object found in walls. But, as in the Hancock-Clarke House jackpot, they have frequently been found along with a wide variety of other items. These have ranged from toys to ears of corn to sleigh bells to spoons.

Hidden shoes have been discovered in walls on both sides of the Atlantic in large enough numbers and in houses far enough distant from one another to eliminate the possibility that the practice was an eccentricity of a particular group of people or confined to a specific region. Yet to date not a single reference to the custom has been found in any written materials.

Perhaps putting a shoe in a wall was a superstition so deeply embedded in tradition that no one even gave a thought to why they were doing it, or deemed it worth documenting in any way—like automatically saying "God bless you" when someone sneezes. Or perhaps a faint aura of pagan superstition still clung to the practice. That, of course, would have run counter to the grain of Christianity, in particular the Puritanism that dominated most of New England for generations. People might have deemed it prudent to perform the custom covertly. Or maybe it was a ritual that according to ancient tradition had to be conducted in secret to ensure its effectiveness.

Present-day scholars have come up with a very important-sounding term for shoes and other articles of clothing discovered in the walls of buildings: deliberately concealed garments. There is even a Deliberately Concealed Garments Project at the Northampton Museum and Art Gallery in England. The project maintains a database that now includes more than two thousand objects, primarily (but by no means exclusively) footwear, that have been found hidden in walls on both sides of the Atlantic. Approximately two hundred of those items were found in the United States, most in New England.

It is both ironic and intriguing that the worn-out shoe, one of the most mundane of possessions, lies at the heart of a major mystery of New England culture. The relatively recent realization of how widespread the practice of hiding shoes in walls was, and the lack of any definitive explanation for it, demonstrate that not only haven't all of New England's mysteries been solved—some haven't even been discovered yet.

BIBLIOGRAPHY

The Darn Man and the Leather Man

Albee, Allison. "The Leather Man." Unpublished ms. Connecticut Historical Society, Hartford, CT.

Botkin, B. A., ed. *A Treasury of New England Folklore*. Rev. ed. New York: American Legacy Press, 1947.

Bowen, Clarence Winthrop. *The History of Woodstock, Connecticut*. Vol. 1. Norwood, MA: Plimpton Press, 1926.

Bristol, Connecticut. Hartford, CT: City Printing, 1907.

"Clad in a Leather Suit: A Curious Character Arrested for Humane Reasons." *New York Times,* December 4, 1888.

Cummiskey, John P. "Do You Recall the Old Leather Man? Mystery of His Life Solved at Last." *Hartford Daily Courant,* March 24, 1935.

Foote, LeRoy W. "Our Connecticut Leather Man." *Lure of the Litchfield Hills,* December 1952.

Globe Museum. *Life of the Mysterious Leather Man, the Wandering Hermit of Connecticut & New York*. New York: New York Popular Publishing, 1889.

Griffith, Lena. Journal. Unpublished ms. Private collection.

Griggs, Susan J. *Folklore and Firesides of Pomfret, Hampton, and Vicinity.* Salem, MA: Higginson Book Company, 1984.

Hartford Courant, October 11, December 12, 1888; January 28, March 26, 1889.

Hegg, Donald M. "Animal Protective Societies." *Dictionary of American History.* Revised edition. Vol. 1. New York: Charles Scribner's Sons, 1976.

"The Leather Man Again: Trying to Unravel the Mystery of His Wanderings." *New York Times,* August 15, 1884.

Lincoln, Allen B., ed. *A Modern History of Windham County, Connecticut.* 2 vols. Chicago: J. S. Clarke Publishing, 1920.

Masters, Al. "Strange Riddle of the Old Leather Man." *New-England Galaxy* 14, no. 3 (Winter 1973).

New York Times, March 22, August 22, 1886; December 8, 1888.

"The 'Old Leather Man.'" *Hartford Daily Courant,* December 4, 1888.

"The Old Leather Man: The Strange Life of an Old Man Clad Entirely in Leather." Clipping from unidentified Connecticut newspaper, ca. 1884.

Penny Press, March 17, April 23, 24, August 23, September 21, November 1, December 3, 6, 12, 1888; February 16, March 25, 1889.

Philips, David E. *Legendary Connecticut: Traditional Tales from the Nutmeg State*. Hartford, CT: Spoonwood Press, 1984.

Sailson, W. A. "The Mystery Solved: The Origin of the Eccentric Leatherman and the Story of His Career." *Hartford Daily Courant*, August 20, 1884.

"Where O.D. Man Died." Unidentified newspaper, Windham County, Connecticut, ca. 1938.

"Zack Boveliat: The Old Leather Man Refuses to Be Taken to the Hospital and Escapes." *Middletown Herald*, December 4, 1888.

"Vampires" in the Family

Barber, John Warner. *Connecticut Historical Collections*. 2nd ed. New Haven, CT: Durrie & Peck and J. W. Barber, 1836.

Belanger, Jeff. "Mercy Brown, the Rhode Island Vampire." www.ghostvillage.com/legends/2003.legends20_06142003 .shtml.

Bell, Michael E. *Food for the Dead: On the Trail of New England's Vampires*. New York: Carroll & Graf, 2001.

"Contagion, Tuberculosis in Europe and North America, 1800–1922." Open Collections Program. http://ocp.hul .harvard.edu.contagion.tuberculosis.html.

"Grave of Mercy L. Brown." www.quahog.org/attractions/index.hp?id=50.

Hartford Daily Courant, May 24, June 16, 1854.

"The Jewett City Vampires." www.geocities.com/hauntedCT/vampires.htm?200815.

Legare, Debbie. "Mercy Brown: New England's Last Vampire." www.suite101.com/print_article.cfm/her_story/83983.

"Old East Cemetery, Willington, Connecticut." www.graveaddiction.com/oldeast.html.

Russell, Gloria. *Westerly Sun.* www.book-of-thoth.com/article390.html.

Sledzik, Paul S., and Nicholas Bellantoni. "Bioarcheological and Biocultural Evidence for the New England Vampire Folk Belief." *American Journal of Physical Anthropology* 94 (1994).

"Tuberculosis." Wikipedia. http://en.wikipedia.org/wiki/Tuberculosis.

U.S. Census. Exeter, Rhode Island. 1880.

U.S. Census. Griswold, Connecticut. 1840.

U.S. Census. Griswold, Connecticut. 1850.

U.S. Census. Griswold, Connecticut. 1860.

"The Willington Vampires: Willington, Connecticut." www
.geocities.com/hauntedCT/vampires2htm?200815.

The Angel of Hadley

"Angel of Hadley." Wikipedia. http://en.wikipedia.org/wiki/
Angel_of_Hadley.

Hutchinson, Thomas. *History of Massachusetts, from the First
Settlement Thereof in 1628, until the Year 1750.* 3rd ed.
2 vols. Salem, MA: Thomas C. Cushing for Thomas and
Andrews, 1795.

Judd, Sylvester. *History of Hadley . . . With an Introduction by
George Sheldon.* Springfield, MA: H. R. Huntting, 1905.

Mather, Increase. *A Brief History of the Warr with the Indians in
New-England.* Boston: John Foster, 1676.

Old Hadley Quarter Millennial Celebration, 1909. Springfield,
MA: F. A. Bassette, 1909.

Orians, G. H. "The Angel of Hadley in Fiction." *American
Literature* 4, no. 3 (November 1932): 257–269.

Sargent, M. L. "Thomas Hutchinson, Ezra Stiles, and the
Legend of the Regicides." *William and Mary Quarterly,* 3rd
series, 49 (1992): 431–448.

Sheldon, George. "The Traditionary Story of the Attack upon Hadley and the Appearance of Gen. Goffe, Sept. 1, 1675: Has It Any Foundation in Fact?" *New England Historical and Genealogical Register* 28 (October 1874): 379–391.

Stiles, Ezra. *A History of Three of the Judges of King Charles I.* Hartford, CT: Elisha Babcock, 1794.

"William Goffe." Wikipedia. http://en.wikipedia.org/wiki/ William_Goffe.

Wilson, Douglas C. "Web of Secrecy: Goffe, Whalley, and the Legend of Hadley." *New England Quarterly* 60, no. 4 (December 1987): 515–548.

The Mystery Stone

Brown, Janice. "The Mystery Stone and Seneca Ladd of Meredith, New Hampshire." Cow Hampshire. http://cowhampshire.blogharbor.com/blog_ archives/2006/10/21/2429293.html.

"Cardiff Giant." Museum of Hoaxes. www.museumofhoaxes .com/hoax/Hoaxipedia/Cardiff_Giant.

"Cardiff Giant." Wikipedia. http://en.wikipedia.org/wiki/ Cardiff_Giant.

"Lake Winnipesaukee Mystery Stone." Wikipedia. http:// en.wikipedia.org/wiki/Lake_Winnipesaukee_mystery_stone.

"The 'Mystery Stone.'" Museum of New Hampshire History. www.nhhistory.org/museumexhibits/mysterystone/mysterystone.htm.

"New England's 'Mystery Stone.'" www.cbsnews.com/stories/2006/07/21/national/printable1826460.shtml.

Nunatsiaw News. www.nunatsiaq.com/archives/60811/news/nunavut/60811_06.html.

The Maine Coon Cat

Cat Fanciers' Association. www.cfa.org/.

Kus, Beth. "Maine Coon Cats Maine Origin Authenticated." The Maine Coon Heritage Site. www.pawpeds.com/MCO/mcsh/articles/maineorig.html.

"The Maine Coon." American Cat Fanciers Association. www.acfacat.com/maine_coon_synopsis.htm.

"Maine Coon." Wikipedia. http://en.wikipedia.org/wiki/Maine_Coon.

The Maine Coon: Cat Breed FAQ. www.fanciers.com/breed-faqs/maine-coon-faq.html.

Maine Coon Rescue. www.mainecoonrescue.net/history.html.

New York Times, May 9, 10, 1895.

Simpson, Frances. *The Book of the Cat.* London: Cassell and Company, 1903.

"State Cat—Maine Coon Cat." Maine Secretary of State Kids. www.maine.gov/sos/kids/about/symbols/cat.htm.

Premature Burial Terror

Bondeson, Jan. *Buried Alive: The Terrifying History of Our Most Primal Fear.* New York: Norton, 2001.

"Buried Alive: A Body Consigned to the Grave Comes to Life in the Coffin." *Fitchburg Daily Sentinel,* October 30, 1890.

"Buried Alive—A Distressing Case." *Berkshire County Eagle,* April 2, 1858.

"Buried Alive in New Haven, Vermont?" www.vermonter.com/evergreen.asp.

Middlebury College, Middlebury, Vermont. "Catalog of the Graduates of Middlebury College." www.archive.org/stream/catalogueofgrad00inmidd/catalogueofgradu00inmidd_djvu.txt.

Nickell, Joe. *Skeptical Inquirer,* March–April 2008. www.csicop.org/si/2008-02/nickell.html.

North American Review 1, no. 1 (May 1815).

Poe, Edgar Allan. "The Premature Burial." http://poestories.com/print/premature.

Tebb, William, and Edward Perry Vollum. *Premature Burial and How It May Be Prevented.* 2nd ed. Edited by Walter R. Hadwen. London: Swan Sonnenschein, 1905.

Phantom Ships

American Advocate and Kennebec Advertiser, Hallowell, Maine, March 2, 1816.

Bacon, Edgar Mayhew. *Narragansett Bay, Its Historic and Romantic Associations.* New York: Knickerbocker Press, 1904.

Barber, John Warner. *Connecticut Historical Collections.* 2nd ed. New Haven: Durrie & Peck and Barber, 1836.

Battery Steele. www.ww2f.com/military-history/18348-pictures-1812-war.html.

Bell, Michael. "The Legend of the Palatine." www.quahog.org/factsfolklore/index.php?id=92.

Boston Daily Advertiser, February 28, 1816.

Boston Gazette, March 13, 1815.

"Burning of the Palatine." *New York Times,* August 15, 1885.

Cameron, Cal. "Benign Souls Return." *Lowell Independent,* October 28, 1959.

"The Dash and the Dead Ship Harpswell." www.unsolvedmysteries.com/usm335596.html.

"Dash Privateer." *American Advocate and Kennebec Advertiser,* Hallowell, Maine, January 14, 1815.

Essex Register, Salem, Massachusetts, January 11, 1815.

Goold, William. *Portland in the Past.* Portland, ME: B. Thurston and Co. for the author, 1886.

Livermore, Samuel Truesdale. *Block Island. I. A Map and Guide. II. A History (Abridged).* Hartford, CT: Case, Lockwood, and Brainard, 1882.

Mather, Cotton. *Magnalia Christi Americana.* London: T. Parkhurst, 1702.

Maule, Elizabeth S., and Randall Wade Thomas. "The Story of *Dash.*" Freeport [Maine] Historical Society *Newsletter,* Summer 2004.

New-England Palladium & Commercial Advertiser, Boston, Massachusetts, January 24, 1815.

"The Phantom Ship." The Society of Colonial Wars in the State of Connecticut. www.colonialwarsct.org/1644htm.

"Phantom Ship." www.nhharbor.net.articles.Great%20Ship%20and%20Phantom%20Ship-1/Phantom%20Ship.htm.

"The Phantom Ship, (sculpture)." Smithsonian American Art Museum. Art Inventories Catalog. Smithsonian Institution Research Information System. http://siris-artinventories.si.edu/ipac20/ipac.jsp?uri=full=3100001~!311737!0.

Whittier, John Greenleaf. "The Dead Ship of Harpswell." http://home.comcast.net/~debee2/NNNS/Harpswell.html.

———. "The Palatine." www.readbookonline.net/readOnLine/8297/.

Zuckerman, Elizabeth. "Legend of 18th-Century Ship Still Haunts Block Island." *Boston Globe,* December 20, 2004.

Colonial "Flyer"

Bell, J. L. "John Childs Promises to Fly from Old North Church." Boston 1775. http://boston1775.blogspot.com/2007/04/john-childs-promises-to-fly-from-old.html.

———. "John Childs, Rope Flyer." Boston 1775. http://boston1775.blogspot.com/2007/04/john-childs-rope-flyer.html.

———. "Mysteries of John Childs." Boston 1775. http://boston1775.blogspot.com/2007/04/mysteries-of-john-childs.html.

Benes, Peter, and Jane Montague Benes, eds. *Itinerancy in New England and New York.* Annual Proceedings, Dublin Seminar for New England Folklore, 1984. Concord, MA: Boston University, 1986.

Boston Gazette, and Country Journal, September 12, 1757.

Boston Weekly News-Letter, September 8 to September 15, 1757.

Breck, Samuel. *Recollections of Samuel Breck*. Edited by
H. E. Scudder. London: Sampson Low, Marston, Searle,
& Rivington, 1877.

"Chronology of Massachusetts Aviation 'Firsts.'" www.massaero
history.org/AF-1757-1957.htm.

"First Human Flight in America." www.celebrateboston.com/
firsts/humanflight.htm.

"First Transcontinental Nonstop Flight." www.national
museum.af.mil/factsheets/factsheet.asp?id=740.

New-Hampshire Gazette, September 23, 1757.

New York Gazette, September 26, 1757.

"North End & Charlestown Walking Tour, Boston,
Massachusetts." New England Travel Planner. http://
newenglandtravelplanner.com/go/ma/boston/sights/walk2
.html.

"Old North Church, North End, Boston, Massachusetts."
www.newenglandtravelplanner.com/go/ma/boston/sights/
old_n_church.html.

Pennsylvania Gazette, September 29, 1757.

Southwark Fair. Cincinnati Art Museum. www.cincinnati
artmuseum.org/Search/collectionsresultsitemdetail.aspx?
OID=94920.

Medium Rising

Burr, Franklin. "A Few Words on an Unpopular Subject." *Hartford Daily Times,* August 10, 1852.

"Daniel Dunglas Home." Wikipedia. http://en.wikipedia.org/wiki/Daniel_Dunglas_Home.

Edmonds, I. G. *D. D. Home: The Man Who Talked with Ghosts.* Nashville, TN: Thomas Nelson, 1978.

Grant, Ellsworth S. *Yankee Dreamers and Doers.* Chester, CT: Pequot Press, 1976.

Home, Daniel Dunglas. *Incidents in My Life.* With an Introduction by Judge Edmonds. 5th ed. New York: 1864. www.spiritwritings.com/incidentsinmylife.pdf.

Captain Kidd's Treasure

"Block Island Legends." *New York Times,* October 19, 1884.

"Captain Kidd: Pirate's Treasure Buried in the Connecticut River." www.bio.umass.edu/biology/conn.river/kidd.html.

"Casco Bay's Buried Treasure." www.historyaliveinme.com/A559A5/historyaliveinme.nsf/folklore/3CA0C030928C0FA286256EC400623D5D?Opendocument.

Ford, George Hare. *Historical Sketches of the Town of Milford.* New Haven, CT: Tuttle, Morehouse and Taylor, 1914.

"Is This Kidd's Treasure?" *New York Times,* February 16, 1884.

Ritchie, Robert C. *Captain Kidd and the War against the Pirates.* Cambridge, MA: Harvard University Press, 1986.

Temple, Josiah Howard. *History of the Town of Palmer, Massachusetts.* Springfield, MA: Town of Palmer, 1889.

Temple, Josiah Howard, and George Sheldon. *A History of the Town of Northfield, Massachusetts, for 150 Years.* Albany, NY: Joel Munsell, 1875.

"The Ultimate Captain William Kidd Web Site." www .captainkidd.pwp.blueyonder.co.uk/index.htm.

Zacks, Richard. *The Pirate Hunter: The True Story of Captain Kidd.* New York: Hyperion, 2002.

Zwicker, Roxie J. *Haunted Portland: From Pirates to Ghost Brides.* Charleston, SC: History Press, 2007.

Champ

"Cape Ann Serpent on Lake Champlain." *Plattsburgh Republican,* July 24, 1819.

"Champ, the Famed Monster of Lake Champlain." Lake Champlain Land Trust. www.lclt.org/Champ.htm.

"Champ (legend)." Wikipedia. http://en.wikipedia.org/wiki/ Champ_28%legend%29.

Chorvinsky, Mark. "'Champ' of Lake Champlain." www
.strangemag.com/champ.html.

"Coelacanth." Wikipedia. http://en.wikipedia.org/wiki/
Coelacanth.

"Lake Champlain's 'Champ.'" www.genesispark.com/genpark/
champ/champ.htm.

McKinstry, Lohr. "Lake Champlain Expedition Searches for
Champy." September 28, 2008. www.pressrepublican.com/
archivesearch/local_story_272053009.html.

Nickell, Joe. "Legend of the Lake Champlain Monster."
Skeptical Inquirer, July 2003. www.csicop.org/si/2003-07/i-
files.html.

Radford, Benjamin. "The Measure of a Monster: Investigating
the Champ Photo." *Skeptical Inquirer,* July 2003. www
.csicop.org/si/2003-07/monster.html.

The Charter Oak

Barber, John Warner. *Historical Scenes in the United States.*
New Haven, CT: Treadway and Adams, 1827.

Bates, Albert Carlos. *Charter Oak.* Hartford, CT: Case,
Lockwood & Brainard, 1907.

———. *The Charter of Connecticut: A Study.* Hartford, CT:
The Connecticut Historical Society, 1932.

Bickford, Christopher B. "Connecticut and Its Charter." The Connecticut Historical Society *Bulletin* 49, no. 3 (Summer 1984).

"Champion Trees." Bushnell Park Foundation, Hartford, CT. www.bushnellpark.org/Content/and_34_Champion_ Treesand_34_.asp.

"Checklist of Selected Objects from the Exhibition 'Charter Oak: Seed of Liberty.'" The Connecticut Historical Society *Bulletin* 49, no. 3 (Summer 1984).

"Connecticut State Capitol and Legislative Office Building." Connecticut General Assembly, Hartford, CT. www.cga.ct .gov/html/citizen/capitolpicturebook.pdf.

Crofut, Florence S. M. *Guide to the History and Historic Sites of Connecticut.* 2 vols. New Haven, CT: Yale University Press, 1938.

Dilella, Steve. "Charter Oak Seedlings." Research Report, April 29, 2005. State of Connecticut. General Assembly. Office of Legislative Research. http://worldcat.org/arcviewer/1/ CZL/2005/05/18/0000011017/viewer/file1.html.

Holmes, Abiel. *American Annals, 1805.* Cambridge, MA: W. Hilliard, 1805.

"Liberties and Legends." Museum of Connecticut History, Connecticut State Library, Hartford, CT. www.museum ofcthistory.org/liberties.asp.

McCain, Diana Ross. "The Ol' Oak Tree." *Connecticut,* November 1987.

Morse, Jedidiah. *The American Geography.* Shepherd Kollock for the author, 1789.

Trent, Robert F. "The Charter Oak Artifacts." The Connecticut Historical Society *Bulletin* 49, no. 3 (Summer 1984).

Trumbull, Benjamin. *A Complete History of Connecticut.* 2 vols. Hartford, CT: Hudson and Goodwin, 1797.

Twain, Mark. "Mark Twain on His Travels." *Alta California,* March 3, 1868. www.twainquotes.com/28680303.html.

Wolcott, Roger. *A Memoir for the History of Connecticut, 1759.* The Connecticut Historical Society *Collections.* Vol. 3. Hartford: Published for the Society, 1895.

Hidden in the Walls

Bell, J. "Shoes Found in Hancock-Clarke Wall." Boston 1775. http://boston1775.blogspot.com/2008/05/shoes-found-in-hancock-clarke-wall.html.

"The Crispin Colloquy, archive 1-25." The Honourable Cordwainers' Company. http://thehcc.org/discus/messages/4/7770.html?1140202338.

Dixon-Smith, Denise. "Concealed Shoes." *Archaeological Leather Group Newsletter,* no. 6 (Spring 1990).

"History of the House." Ward-Heitman House Museum. www .wardheitmann.org/history.html.

"If These Walls Could Talk: Concealed Shoes at Sycamores." Sycamores House. www.sycamoreshouse.org/Concealed_ Shoes.html.

"Ightham Mote Kent: Hidden Shoes." www.channel4.com/ history/microsites/T/timeteam/2004/ightham_shoes.html.

McAvoy, Marge. "Collections Connections." Sharon [Connecticut] Historical Society *Newsletter* (Spring 2005). www.sharonhist.org/newsletterspring2005.htm.

Murphy, Ian B. "Renovators Do Some Sole Searching." *Lexington Minuteman*, May 1, 2008.

"Pilgrim Resources." Alden House Historic Site. www.alden .org/pilgrim_lore/pilgrimquiz.htm.

"Shoes in the Wall." Wayland [Massachusetts] Historical Society. http://wayhistsoc.home.comcast.net/~wayhistsoc/ whs/Shoes_in_the_Wall/shoes_in_the_wall.htm.

Swann, June. "Shoes Concealed in Buildings." *Costume,* no. 30, 1996.

"What Is a Deliberately Concealed Garment?" Deliberately
Concealed Garments Project. www.concealedgarments.org/
information/what_dcg.html.

INDEX

ABOUT THE AUTHOR

Historian Diana Ross McCain has been writing about Connecticut's past for more than twenty-five years. She holds bachelor's and master's degrees in history. She is the author of *To All on Equal Terms: The Life and Legacy of Prudence Crandall,* the award-winning biography of Connecticut's official state heroine; *It Happened in Connecticut;* and *Connecticut Coast: A Town-by-Town Illustrated History.* She lives in Durham, Connecticut.